DENAVIBVS · ET

the
VIKINGS

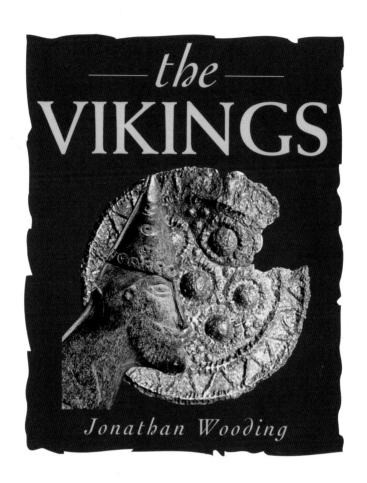

Jonathan Wooding

RIZZOLI
NEW YORK

Contents

Introduction

The Vikings have always had a dramatic image — this has been at once a hindrance and a help to our appreciation of their contribution to history. Hagar the Horrible and his ilk continue to remind us of the Viking raids upon the centres of European culture.

Soon after these raids had ended, however, it is less often remembered that Viking *settlers* proved themselves to be as cultured and enterprising as any people in European history. They are remembered as unwelcome aliens in many countries — yet the people of these same countries are often descended from Vikings and owe many aspects of their civilisation to their Viking ancestry.

Those who have looked closely at the Vikings have found much to admire. Writers from Sir Walter Scott to C.S. Lewis have been inspired by their myths. Much modern design, including Liberty print (designed by the Manxman, Archibald Knox), owes inspiration to their beautiful art. The Icelandic descendants of the Vikings anticipated Columbus' discovery of America by 500 years. Their ideas of freedom and self-determination inspired many of the political ideas of the twentieth century.

In the inclusive climate of today we are more and more able to appreciate the diversity and brilliance which the Viking Age brought to western civilisation. This book aims to show the Vikings as *people* — individual, creative and humane.

The extent of Viking settlement in the 9th and 10th centuries.

"A Fierce, Wrathful, Purely Pagan Folk"

So wrote the monks of an Ireland ravaged by Vikings. This brutal image of the Vikings remains today, though museums and archeological sites now also show us Vikings who were traders, manufacturers and explorers. Who were these Vikings? What were their origins? And why did they sail from their Scandinavian homeland?

Coastal Raiders — the Vikings

To the English, Irish and French writers of the ninth century AD, the Vikings were not nice people. Over a period of around 80 years, coastal and riverside towns across western Europe were subjected to brutal raids by sea-borne marauders. Contemporary writers usually referred to them as "Northmen" and quickly recognised them as being from the Scandinavian countries which lay across the North Sea. Today we refer to these raiders as *Vikings*, rather than "Northmen", using the name given them by the Old Norse writers of the twelfth and thirteenth centuries AD.

Viking isn't really a contemporary name, though it may have been used earlier than our first references to it. The origin of the word is not fully known. In the language of the Norwegian Vikings, Old Norse, *vík* means a salty inlet of the sea, or a "creek". So presumably the name Viking carries some sense of coastal raiding or setting out to sea. We can't say anything more precise than that.

A Significant Contribution

We have no doubt as to who the Vikings were. Starting with the first raids in the late 700s and their ever-increasing settling abroad after the 850s, the Vikings' particular style of settlement and economy saw them remain a distinct element in the populations of areas such as England, Ireland, Russia and the Baltic States for over three centuries, as well as leaving long-term colonies in Iceland and Greenland.

In the course of this activity, the Vikings introduced a sophisticated urban economy, a beautiful series of art styles and a robust communication system to Europe. After the event, we also have come to appreciate the richness of their literary culture, preserved in the Viking colony of Iceland. And we especially admire the range of their exploration and settlement, which saw them establish colonies stretching right across the North Atlantic to Greenland and America.

Straight away we see that the Vikings combined some very impressive

▶ *Viking sword from Hedeby, Denmark. This artefact symbolises the conflicting images of the Viking Age. Though from a commercial centre, it is a tool of conflict as well as an object of beauty, with delicate designs in gold and silver.*

achievements with violent abuses of the people they came among. This dichotomy presents a dilemma for many people who study them: should we admire or revile these people?

A Question of Points of View

The Vikings were more or less unknown foreigners when they arrived in western Europe. They were of impressive size and appearance. They were also pagan and illiterate. This is important when we consider how often hatred of incoming groups can be a matter of ideology. The Christian writers of western Europe felt free to discriminate against these foreigners. Because they could not write, the Vikings have not left their own side of the story.

Many Vikings were probably refugees from political and social upheaval in Scandinavia. Like many refugee or migrant groups, they were not easily accepted abroad. This is not to say that they didn't do many despicable things. But they were scarcely the only ethnic group to pillage monasteries or burn towns in the ninth century AD, and probably, as non-Christians, were attributed with many crimes that others committed.

◀ *Axe from a Danish burial at Mammen. Dating from the 10th century, this axe is decorated in what has come to be known as the Mammen Style (see chapter 8). The distinctive pattern was created by inlaying it with silver wire.*

⊛ *Political Unrest in Scandinavia* ⊛

The upheavals in Scandinavia which caused the Vikings to plunder and, later, to settle abroad were the direct result of increased contact with western Europe. Under Charlemagne, the empire had expanded to the borders of Denmark and was now exerting a new political influence in Scandinavia.

▼ *Geiranger Fjord, on Norway's west coast. Along this coast ancient trading and communication routes stretch from the Arctic hunting lands to the markets of Europe in the south. Conflict and competition between the small maritime kingdoms which existed deep in such fjords was a prelude to the extended piracy of the Viking Age.*

Scandinavia had remained at some distance from the events of the Roman Empire and its successor states. In the late 700s AD Scandinavia was still a pagan Germanic society, a collection of Iron Age petty kingdoms trading only indirectly with the lands to the south. All this began to change with the Frankish conquest of Germany. This brought a Romanised, Christian civilisation into close proximity to Denmark.

It is likely that contact with Christian culture was responsible for the rise of Scandinavian kings who had more imperialist ideas. These kings united larger kingdoms by force and regulated trade. Such regulation of a dispersed society inevitably caused displacement of minor royalty, isolating free traders and turning them into "pirates". It was these displaced groups who we suspect suddenly began to look abroad — first to supplement their failing social position, then to find new lands elsewhere in Europe.

God's Scourge or Displaced Persons?

The raids, the pillaging and the cruelties inflicted on their victims may tempt us to follow their contemporaries in seeing the Vikings as a scourge, an expression of God's moral anger upon the sinful Europeans. In fact, while we shouldn't apologise for the violence committed by the Vikings, we cannot condemn a whole civilisation on the strength of a period of upheaval. Their situation is very similar to that of the refugee in modern Europe, who is also often fleeing from a society in which the West has interfered politically and upset the old political order. Whatever its cause, the raids of the Vikings were human actions, in response to human dramas in Scandinavia.

A Dramatic Entrance — the First Raids

The first Viking raid was in 793 upon Lindisfarne, near the Scottish border on England's east coast. Nearby Jarrow was raided the following year and the monastery of Iona, on the west coast of Scotland, was sacked in 795. Rathlin Island, off Ireland's north coast, was raided in the same year. By 799 the Vikings were raiding western France.

"793: then severe foreboding came over Northumbria and people were cruelly terrified; there were immense lightening flashes and fiery dragons were seen flying in the air. Then came a great famine; and after these came a little later the heathens' harrying which destroyed God's church in the island of Lindisfarne with rape and slaughter."

The Anglo-Saxon Chronicle.

▲ *This medieval gravestone was found in the cemetery at Lindisfarne. It is thought to commemorate the Viking raids, though it is obviously not a contemporary snapshot.*

Many of these raids were upon monasteries, which were situated on small islands off the coast. Lindisfarne and Iona held magnificent collections of saints' relics — such as the remarkable manuscripts the *Lindisfarne Gospels* and the *Book of Kells*, as well as rich collections of metalwork.

Probably it was the metalwork which the raiders were after, but by choosing to sack these centres of learning and writing the Vikings earned their reputation as despoilers of western civilisation. Sacking centres of written culture also ensured that the Vikings would be remembered. These monasteries were the communications centres of their era.

The Lindisfarne raid appears to have been more or less out of the blue. We know now that the Vikings had probably already colonised the Shetland and Orkney islands in the previous few years. The picture created in the sources is that of audacious, commando-style raiders. Images of the savagery of the raids abound in both the contemporary reports and in the literature written by their Icelandic successors.

Monkish chroniclers speculated on whether God was punishing the Christian peoples for some fault, and kings and nobles racked their brains in an attempt to come up with a strategy which could defeat the Vikings.

Ermentarius of Noirmoutier, writing in the 860s, expresses this helplessness: "There is a ceaseless flood of Northmen. Christians are massacred, burnt and despoiled everywhere... Countless ships travel up the Seine and evil spreads throughout the region."

Ermentarius was a fit person to write down such grievances. Thirty years earlier, his own monastery, that of St Philibert at Noirmoutier, off the west coast of France near Nantes, was sacked and the monks were obliged to flee, carrying the relics of their founder saint with them.

The Vikings were not always victorious. In 844 AD Abd-al-Rahman II, the ruler of Islamic Spain, took hundreds of Vikings prisoner and hanged them, and the city's trees are said to have born "unusual fruit".

◀ *A page from the magnificent* Book of Kells. *This beautiful illuminated manuscript of the Gospels may have been in the process of being made at Iona when the monastery was raided by the Vikings in 795. It was removed to the monastery of Kells in Ireland and is now in the library of Trinity College in Dublin.*

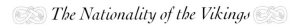
The Nationality of the Vikings

The circumstances surrounding the entry of the Vikings into the history of western Europe were dramatic. But exactly where did they come from?

The evidence mostly points to the earliest raiders being Norwegian in origin. Scandinavia, in the late 700s, seems to have just been beginning to separate into the sorts of settlement and cultural divisions which make up the distinction between Norwegians, Swedes and Danes today. These three nations are very similar in culture and would have spoken very similar dialects in the Viking period. Often Swedes would be found among Norwegian communities, such as in ninth-century Iceland. Likewise, though Russia was mostly colonised by Swedish Vikings, the Norwegian king Harald Hardrada was active there in the eleventh century.

Into Russia

While the entry into western Europe was violent and dramatic, the Vikings at the same time seem to have been migrating into Russia in a much less obtrusive fashion. The Russian *Primary Chronicle* of the fourteenth century talks of a violent and dramatic invasion in the 860s, but other sources confirm that this story is most likely just propaganda and Vikings had been arriving in dribs and drabs as early as the 830s.

Conquering England

Danish Vikings seem to have been involved in the earlier raids upon western Europe, but their major role in the history of the Viking Age was to make systematic settlements in the eastern part of England. Danish raiders had been wintering on islands in East Anglia as early as the 830s. After the 860s, when Ivar the Boneless and his brothers conquered the Anglian kingdoms of East Anglia and York, the Danes were a permanent part of the English political landscape. Their lands became known as the Danelaw ("under the laws of the Danes").

England Resists — Alfred the Great

The king of Wessex, Alfred the Great, put a stop to the Scandinavian marauders. Wessex was not a powerful or influential kingdom, and

▲ *Twelfth century tapestry from Baldishol, Norway. This brilliant image is of a mounted warrior involved in warfare on the land — in contrast with the guerilla raiding of the Vikings. The creation of narrative tapestries and embroideries was a feature of medieval Scandinavian art.*

Alfred struggled for a long time without allies or success. He lost his throne to the Danes and was forced to flee into the fen country. In 878 AD, approximately six months after he had been dethroned, his messengers had summoned a great army of English. Alfred picked his moment with care: the men of Devon, under Odda, were resisting Guthrum and the Danes, so Alfred fought an already weary army and defeated them. He insisted that the Danes convert to Christianity, and thus secured a treaty between fellow Christians under the same God.

▲ *Horses being unloaded from ships — illustration from the Bayeux Tapestry. This textile, made in the late 11th century, depicts ships which are certainly of Viking type — though they are actually the ships of the Vikings' Norman descendents. The multi-coloured use of thread is used to depict the overlapping planks of the clinker-building method. The animal heads on the prows are paralleled on the walking stick from Bergen in the picture opposite.*

From Northmen to Normans

In France, a mixture of Danish and Norwegian Vikings settled in the Frankish province of Neustria, which was renamed Normandy (from *normenn* — "northmen"). These Normans soon became French-speaking. Nonetheless, their material culture and their histories reflect a consciousness of their Viking origins. The Norman ships depicted in the Bayeux Tapestry, for example, are very like the Viking longships recovered from Scandinavian sites.

Vikings — a Major Cultural Influence

The Vikings are therefore a considerable component in the ethnic history of England, Ireland, Russia, Iceland and France, among other nations. This has considerably affected the historical treatment of them. In Ireland they are mainly portrayed as a foreign threat to the Irish identity. In Russia they have been depicted as the founders of the modern Russian state — *Rus* or *Rhos* was indeed originally a term for "Scandinavian" in Russia.

Such claims have more to do with modern politics than with history. In both Ireland and Russia the Vikings in fact seem to have lived as traders in their own towns, which were separate to contemporary kingdoms in those regions. Nonetheless they are a part of the ethnic history of those nations, not something alien to them. In England, the public interest in the excavation of the Viking town of York (*Jorvík*) represents the reinclusion of the Vikings into the history of England in their urban, commercial role — an image with which the modern person can identify.

▼ *Vikings fleet — inscription on a stick from Bergen, Norway. The harbour of Bergen in the Viking era would have been crowded with longships and other craft. This sketch on the shaft of a walking stick has preserved a glimpse of the harbour during these times. Note the animal figureheads and triangular wind vanes.*

▲ The Althing — *this romantic painting by the pre-Raphaelite artist W.G. Collingwood depicts the medieval parliament of Iceland. Collingwood was one of many 19th-century romantics (the designer William Morris was another) who saw Iceland as an ideal democracy and the Vikings as rugged medieval socialists.*

▲ *Sonderala vane. This beautiful gilt weather vane is decorated in the Urnes Style of the 11th century. It once would have graced the stempost of a Viking ship. It has been preserved because it was subsequently used as a weather vane on a church.*

Violence — a Matter of Perception?

The tendency to cast the Vikings in a negative and destructive role is the result of a couple of curious circumstances. We first of all must appreciate that, while in our era we do not admire violence as an expression of free-spiritedness and independence, not all past people felt the same way.

The Vikings' own descendants, the Icelanders, created an image of the Vikings in their novels, or *sagas* (from the Old Norse word for "speech") in which brutal violence was combined with heroic independence of spirit and even literary gifts. Egil Skallagrimson, the hero of *Egils Saga* is one such "poet warrior" figure. But the image created by fourteenth-century descendants of the Vikings is no more than a literary image and may not do justice to the values of ninth-century Vikings.

The dynamic energy of the Vikings as explorers, traders and artists was not the result of primitive and rapacious urges. Sagas depict Vikings as cunning and crafty people. Eirik the Red, for example, in attempting to promote colonisation in Greenland in the 980s, is said to have given it the name "Greenland", because "people would want to go there if it had a nice name". But this is a literary tale, written years later and may be no more true than the Hollywood image of a businessman who says "greed is good".

In their desire to find rugged northern individualists, the social idealists of the 19th century pre-Raphaelite movement created our modern image of the Viking, by conflating literary sources with reality. The consequence was the image of proud, overbearing Germanic warriors which underpinned the ideology of Nazi Germany — this means there are good reasons to bury the "poet-warrior" myth.

"Viking" — a Household Name

The word "Viking" has come to be applied to such diverse achievements as the brilliant literary civilisation of the Scandinavian colony in Iceland, to the travellers who visited Russia, Byzantium, North America, Greenland and the high Arctic, and to the impressive mercantile exploits which built an enormous trade network across Northern Europe. Icelandic literature has found a place in the English Departments of most universities. Thor the Thunder God is a Marvel Comics hero, and Hagar the Horrible has graced our newspapers for some years. The Vikings are a household name in our society.

"Iron Studded Snakes" — Viking Ships

Sorrow will be the lot of men,
before the drawing in of the seventy oars from sea
Northmen row this iron-studded snake downstream.
Waves part like the shape of eagles' wings.

Heimskringla, Snorri Sturluson

The Ship — Symbol of the Vikings

The Viking ship is the classic symbol of Viking civilisation. Its elegance and technical sophistication symbolise the high standard of Viking craftsmanship. It made possible their travels from Scandinavia to raid, colonise and explore the Northern World.

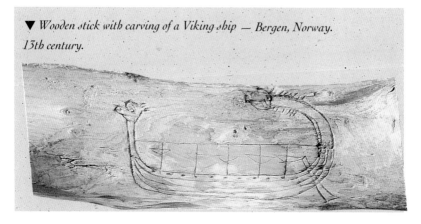

▼ *Wooden stick with carving of a Viking ship — Bergen, Norway. 13th century.*

◀ *Carved wooden bedpost from the Oseberg ship burial —
by an artist nicknamed the "Academian". The ship burial
at Oseberg is a royal tomb of great richness. A pair of
bedposts from Oseberg marks the cultural and
technological change in the mid 9th century — the
transition from Migration period art and technology to
the very refined work of the Viking era.*

Viking ships were long and narrow. They were pointed at both ends
(what is known as "double ended") and built from narrow planks, each
slightly overlapping the one below (called *clinker* building). The planks
curved up at each end to be joined onto the posts at the front ("bow")
and rear ("stern"). These posts were often adorned with carvings of
animal's heads or other elaborate images.

The Viking warship or "longship" (*langskip* in Old Norse) had no deck
and was an open boat, looking rather like a modern surfboat. The smaller
trading and exploring ship, known in Old Norse as a *knörr*, had decking
over part of its length. This was necessary to keep cargo dry. Both types of
ships carried sails, but we think that the longship was mostly rowed,
with the sail only used when the wind was directly behind the ship.

In battle, rowing is an important means of propulsion. The ship
must be able to be manoeuvred into attacking positions, or out of the

line of fire, quickly. There is no time to wait for the wind to change. A trading ship, on the other hand, needs cargo space and it cannot afford to employ too many crew, as this would lower profits from the voyage. The knörr therefore only carried a few oars, for manoeuvring in and out of harbour and near the shore. Steering was controlled by a side rudder. To us, this would appear more like another oar than a modern rudder.

Viking ships do not resemble our idea of a "ship". They are far more substantial, however, than the large rowboats which they appear to be at first glance. These were the vessels in which Viking mariners sailed to all parts of Europe, into the Mediterranean, to the High Arctic and across the Atlantic to Greenland and North America. In this latter case the ships in which the Viking explorers sailed were arguably more suited to their task than those used by Columbus five centuries later. Replicas of Viking ships have been built to prove this point.

▶ *The Gokstad ship. From a mid 9th-century burial in Norway, probably a royal burial of the Vestfold dynasty this, our finest example of a longship, was preserved by being buried in a pocket of clay which was rich in organic matter. A replica of this ship was sailed to the World's Fair in Chicago in 1893.*

▲ *In this picture from the late 11th-century Bayeux Tapestry, Viking-style longships are depicted carrying William the Conqueror's Norman army to Britain in 1066. Note the side rudders, similar to that on the Oseberg ship opposite.*

In 1893 one such replica crossed from Norway to North America in only twenty-eight days, doing speeds of up to ten and eleven knots in the process. With an experienced Viking crew it presumably would have made the crossing even more easily. This ship was a full scale replica of the elegant vessel dug from a burial mound at Gokstad in the Oslo Fjord in 1880. A perfectly preserved longship, 23m (76 feet) in length and 5.2m (17 feet) in width, it is one of the most beautiful artefacts ever turned up by the excavator's spade. Its simple beauty is matched to some degree by the more elaborately carved vessel of similar dimensions (70 feet by 17 feet) dug from a burial mound at Oseberg, only a few miles away, in 1904. Both of these ships are probably ninth century in date.

That these two ships of the longship class have become symbolic of the Viking seafaring achievement is the result of a misconception. For it was not in the longship, but in the shorter and broader knörr, that the Vikings made the bulk of their long distance voyages to places such as Greenland and America. No archeological find of a knörr was made, however, until 1962 when an excavation at the mouth of Roskilde Fjord in Denmark uncovered several ships which had been sunk to block the harbour mouth in an eleventh-century naval action. One of these was a knörr, some 16.1m (53 feet) long and 4.5m (15 feet) in breadth. A reconstruction of this vessel named *Saga Siglar* ("saga sailor") sailed around the world in 1985.

Ships' Construction

Though the knörr was shorter than the longship, it nonetheless embodied the same design features which were the strengths of the longship. Clinker-built ships were not constructed in the way in which most wooden ships have been built over recent centuries, that is by setting up a framework of internal ribs to give the vessel its initial shape. The clinker-built vessel is made by first fastening each plank to the next, from the bottom up, with a row of rivets. Only afterwards are light internal frames added to help the vessel retain its shape. In the Viking ship the outer shell is the actual structure of the ship itself.

◀ *Stern view of the Oseberg Ship. Note the side rudder, a combined oar and rudder which allowed the Vikings to control their ships in the roughest seas. The side rudder was preferred to a fixed rudder owing to the need to draw the rudder out of the water when landing in shallow water, such as on the beach.*

◀ *The Oseberg ship, from a Norwegian burial mound dating back to the 9th century. This beautiful Viking longship comes from a richly furnished burial, probably of a Norwegian queen. The ship itself is finely decorated, with carvings on the stem post, in contrast to the contemporary Gokstad Ship.*

In the conventional, or "carvel"-built vessel, the outer shell is in essence only a "skin" to keep the water out.

The Swedish sea captain Magnus Andersson, while sailing his replica of the Gokstad ship to America in 1893, found that the clinker-built Viking ship behaved quite unusually at sea. Andersson observed that the body of the ship gave with the movement of the sea, with the ship showing such flexibility that the gunwale could twist out of line as much as 15cm (six inches) — all the time staying completely watertight.

When a ship's hull is under one set of pressures from the motion of the waves, the sail may be at the same time being pushed in the other direction by a strong wind. The ability of the sides of the ship to twist and "give" by a matter of a few inches is an immeasurable asset. The danger of the boat breaking under the strain thus becomes reduced and the boat can be made of much lighter materials than if the vessel were to rely upon sheer solidity of construction.

The simplicity of form of most elements of the Viking ship is deceptive. The presence of square sails in most images of Viking ships, and their evidence for use of oars, would suggest that Vikings would only have sailed when there was a following wind. Experiments, especially with the implement known as the *beitiáss*, which allows the edge of the sail to be held out, helping the vessel sail closer to the wind, give us to understand that the Viking knörr was actually very effective in sailing against the wind. Likewise, the oar-like rudder of the Viking ship, despite its simple appearance, was found by Magnus Andersson to be a most effective mechanism. It had the virtue, also, of being able to be lifted from the water when the ship landed on a beach. The stern rudder of modern vessels was only developed when wharfs and dredged channels became common.

The flexibility and strength of Viking ships allowed mariners to survive almost impossibly threatening conditions, sometimes landing safely through fierce surf:

> *There was no other course but to steer onto the shore... they sailed onto the shore and came to land at the Humber mouth; all the men and most of the goods on board were rescued from the ship — but it was broken to pieces.*
>
> **Egils Saga**

Snakelike — Simplicity of Form

This serpentine flexibility of Viking ships may explain the numerous literary comparisons made by the Vikings between ships and snakes. One famous ship of the tenth century was called *Ormrinn Langi* ("the long serpent").

Though the knörr was undoubtedly also very flexible, its rather bluff bow structure inspired a different comparison. Such ships might be described as having "beautiful bosoms" — while a woman might be termed "*knörr*-breasted".

Navigation

The question of the simple Viking navigation techniques has aroused much debate. Land lubberly cultural prejudices have left their mark on this aspect of Viking studies. It has been instantly, and groundlessly, assumed by many scholars that Viking sailors would have only unwillingly ventured out of sight of land. The Kirk Douglas movie, *The Vikings*, is the most public manifestation of a false argument that

Vikings must have possessed magnetic compasses to have sailed out of sight of land. A simple reading of the saga evidence would instantly reveal that the Vikings were, by preference, deep sea sailors and certainly did not possess the magnetic compass.

The scholar who sits at a desk, examining a map, may have no conception of the actual conditions confronting the mariner at sea level. In the northern seas, with the aid of prevailing currents, the indication of relative latitude given by the height of the sun and the pole star, and the ability to steer a straight line with the help of a regular wind and wave pattern, the mariner has no need of a compass. In Arctic waters cloud formations, flight paths of birds and atmospheric projections of images from below the horizon, all make land easy enough to detect from a distance often double the range of the naked eye. Sailors steering by dead reckoning, or "run of the sea", therefore were mostly in little danger of missing their target.

Ships usually only went astray in fog or storm when sailors would

◀ The Lillbjars Stele. This stone is one of a number of the same type on the mid-Baltic island of Gotland. Probably around 7th century in date, it depicts a warrior on horseback in the upper panel and a ship sailing in the bottom panel. It may tell the story of a warrior who is carried to the otherworld by ship.

lose their points of reference and become disoriented. This was what happened to Bjarni Herjolfsson when, late in the tenth century, he set out from Iceland for Greenland. Though blown totally off course to North America he was immediately able to orient himself once the storm had lifted and find his way to Greenland. As he had never before visited Greenland, let alone even heard of America, this was a remarkable demonstration of the degree of control over their element, exercised by the Viking mariners.

A Fine Design

The Viking ship, indeed, represents the greatest refinement of the Germanic ship type. As such it is almost an optimal development in maritime design: one of the finest ship designs of all time. However, in evolutionary terms it represents a dead end. Superbly suited as it was to the geography of the northern seas it did not adapt well to later economic conditions.

When the advent of man-made harbours and dredged channels brought the possibility of larger ships for bulk commerce, the clinker style became obsolete. The carvel-built Mediterranean *carrack*, with its side by side planks, replaced the clinker-built *cog* — the larger, deeper late-medieval incarnation of the knörr. The rigid carvel construction was found to be more suitable for larger vessels. The 16th-century wreck of the warship *Mary Rose* of Henry VIII, recovered from Spithead in 1982, provides an interesting insight in this regard. Examination of the hull shows it to have been originally clinker-built, but later rebuilt as a carrack when required to carry a heavier weight of armaments and to have gun ports cut in the side.

The clinker technique is nowadays used only to build row boats and fishing boats. Yet this should not distract us from its earlier use in the Viking ships. These are undoubtedly deserving of the name "ship" and are among the most refined ships of all time.

Between Fire and Ice — the Doom of the Gods

U ntil the middle of the ninth century, the Vikings were mostly pagans. Like the religions of the pagan Greeks and the Romans, the Viking religion had a series of myths about a set of gods with very human personalities. These included figures such as Thor, Odin and Freyja, whose names are still recognised today. Thor has appeared in our culture as a cartoon hero. Freyja is quite a common girl's name. Odin appears in the operas of Wagner.

The gods of the Vikings seem to have been the same as those of the other early Germanic peoples. The early English peoples of German origin, the Angles and Saxons, for example, had the same gods as the Norse. This can be seen from some of our names for the days of the week, which take their names from the Old English versions of the Norse gods' names: Tuesday is from "Tyr's day"; Wednesday is from "Woden's day" (the same god as the Norse Odin); Thursday is from "Thor's day"; Friday is from "Frigg's day".

It is also clear from illustrations, inscriptions and some literary quotations that many of the early Germanic peoples must have shared the same basic fund of myths about the gods.

▲ *Page from the Icelandic manuscript* Flateyjarbók, *dated to the 13th century. This manuscript is named after the monastery at Flatey in Iceland. Other manuscripts had more descriptive names, such as* Fagrskinna *("fine pages") or* Morkinskinna *("rotten pages"). The illuminated initial depicts a scene from the saga of King Harald Finehair.*

Icelandic Literary Tradition

We begin to understand the importance of the Vikings to the history of western Europe when we consider how little we would know in detail of the beliefs of northern Europeans were it not for the richness of the literary tradition established in Iceland.

It was unusual for an early medieval people to record their own mythology in their own language. Most writing was done by

▲ *A few miles from the Icelandic capital, Reykjavík, the Thingvellir was the site of the Icelandic* Althing, *the national parliament, which met here annually from the 900s until in recent centuries — when it moved to more comfortable premises in the capital. The name is from the Old Norse* thingwöller *("assembly place") which also gave rise to the names* Dingwall *and* Tingwall *in Scotland and* Tynwald, *the assembly place of the Isle of Man.*

churchmen in Latin. Most "vernacular" literature was left in the oral tradition and was eventually forgotten. There is much speculation as to why the Icelanders would have come to write as extensively as they did.

To understand why, we must appreciate the unusual basis of the national identity of the medieval Icelanders.

Indomitable Exiles

Every nation has some point in its past history which is identified as shaping the character of the people. In America, people identify with the Wild West and the Civil War — in Australia they single out their convict origins. The medieval Icelanders looked back to their own Viking forebears, believing that the first settlers had been driven out of Norway by the tyranny of a king called Harald Finehair. This led them to identify with the idea that they were an individualistic and free-minded people because of their origins as political refugees. Icelanders therefore especially idolised their Viking forebears, as people of independent action.

We now know that this is a false picture as the earliest Icelandic colonists must have left Norway before Harald was old enough to tyrannise anyone besides his mother. The truth about their origins didn't stop the Icelanders believing they were independent by character. Probably they were indeed refugees — from a Norway coming under increasingly centralised rule, prior to Harald's reign.

Parliament — the "Althing"

Once in Iceland, the colonists abandoned the monarchical system of Norway and organised their society as a republic with an annual parliament called the Althing — as well as a series of local parliaments to dispense justice. These parliaments, however, were more than just political assemblies. As the greater part of the free people of Iceland (the slaves, a large proportion of the population, were not represented) came to the Althing, they also took the opportunity to conduct athletics meetings and trading fairs.

Politics and Poetry

It was the hobby of Norse nobles to compose court poetry called *Skaldic* verse. These verses were not written down at the time, but learned off by heart. They are allusive and complicated poems. As many of the earliest settlers in Iceland were probably minor rulers who were displaced by the new order, they may have included such poets among their number.

Isolated from mainstream European society, the Icelanders did things their own way. When Iceland converted to Christianity in 1000 AD, the local chieftains became the bishops and most church business was conducted in Icelandic.

It probably took a combination of a low level of literacy in Latin, combined with a strong secular tradition of poetry and storytelling, to create the environment for what was to become a literary outpouring.

Lawspeaker-Poet — Snorri Sturluson

One of Iceland's most gifted and original writers was Snorri Sturluson. In a long and active life, Snorri was elected Lawspeaker (President) of the Althing on three occasions, as well as visiting the Norwegian court. Among his works were a massive history (*Heimskringla* "orb of the world"), one of the most famous novels (*Egils Saga*) and the text we call the Snorri's *Edda*, or "the Younger" *Edda*.

The message of this work is a proud one. European learning was dominated by churchmen, whose major allegiance was to an antique and Christian learning system. Poetry and other writing was of a Classical tradition, full of allusions to Greek and Roman myths.

Snorri was not a churchman, but a rare thing at that time: a literate statesman. Like many well-bred Norsemen, he composed court poetry in Old Norse, not Latin. As Norse poetry too, was full of allusions, not to Classical mythology, but to Norse mythology, he wrote a manual explaining what these myths were and their relevance to interpreting literature — in doing so, he set up his *own* ancient culture as being of equal worth to classical civilisation. It is through this bold work that we have the myths preserved for us.

Reflections of Life on Earth

Tales from Norse mythology tell of the "Doom of the Gods" (Old Norse *Ragnarók*). The Norse gods were not directly involved with the lives of people. Rather, they were caught up in their own complex struggles which reflected upon aspects of life on Midgard ("middle earth" — our own world).

This disengagement of the gods from everyday life wasn't really a problem. A man was more noble if he could fight his way through life and die with a defiant jest upon his lips, with a bravery that was the purer because it was without hope of a reward in the next world. The religion of the Vikings offered no salvation. We suspect the concept of Valhalla, an afterlife for the greatest warriors, is probably a late addition to the mythology, the result of Christian influence. The most valued immortality for a Viking was, in this world, to achieve lasting fame in poetry and song.

 The Creation

The Norse myths are complex and entertaining, whatever their social role. Snorri tells us that in the beginning there was Ginnungagap, a yawning chasm between Muspellheim (the realm of fire) and Niflheim (the realm of ice). Eventually the ice and fire collided and this resulted in the creation of a huge giant called Ymir, and of a cow, Audhumla. The cow licked at the ice to feed herself, and eventually revealed a man, Buri, who was embedded in the ice. Other giants had grown from under Ymir's arms and from between his toes. Buri married a giantess, and their three grandsons, Odin, Vili and Ve slew Ymir and from his body made the world, his blood became the seas and lakes. His flesh became the surface of the earth, his bones became the mountains, and rocks and pebbles were made from the teeth and jaws and any bones that were broken. They flung his brains into the air and they became the clouds. The gods also built a wall from Ymir's eyebrows, making the world into a fortress, called Midgard.

The universe created in this somewhat gory fashion did not stop there. There were nine different worlds or realms, all of which were held together by a giant ash tree called Yggdrasil. This tree had three great roots, one passing into Asgard (the home of the gods), one passing into Jotunheim (the home of the giants), the third of which passed into Hel, the home of the dead. Yggdrasil's trunk went through Midgard, the realm of men. The other five realms are Alfheim and Svartalfheim (homes of the light and dark elves respectively), Vanaheim (home of the Vanir, a secondary family of gods), Muspellheim (the world of fire), and Niflheim (the world of ice).

The Gods — Struggles Against Doom

Great emphasis was placed on individual gods. They were shown to be like humans in many ways. Their exchanges and struggles against their ultimate doom reflected the human condition. Odin was the ruler of the gods, a fearsome figure who constantly hungered for enlightenment. He gave up one of his eyes so he could drink from the Well of Mimir. He seduced a giant girl to gain access to the mead of poetic inspiration and underwent crucifixion, in order to gain knowledge of secret runes. This is described in the *Hávamál*:

> *I know that I hung exposed to the wind*
> *Nine nights in all, wounded by the spear*
> *and given to Odin.*
> *Myself given to myself on that tree*
> *of which no man knows where its roots run.*
> *They did not bless me with loaf or horn.*
> *I looked down, took up the runes,*
> *Shrieking I took them, then I fell.*

The wisdom which Odin gained from this somewhat suspiciously Christ-like experience allowed him knowledge of the future, where he could see the

◀ *Bronze statuette of Thor. Thor was undoubtably the most popular god among ordinary Vikings. A large number of statuettes survive of Thor from domestic contexts. This 10th-century statuette was found in Iceland.*

ultimate doom of the gods. Many of the adventures of the gods are involved with attempts to stave off the final doom.

The commonness of statues of Thor, and of his name in place and personal name-giving, shows that he was the most popular of the gods for folk worship. Thor is depicted as a huge ruddy-faced peasant. His magic hammer Mjollnir generated the lightning and the thunder.

Thor's sidekick, Loki, actually was a giant, not a god. He was so clever and attractive that Odin made him a blood-brother. Loki's presence brought the gods into contact with the giants, however, and this hastened their ultimate destruction.

The giants were the enemies of the gods. Many of the myths centre on adventures involving the gods and the giants. The hammer of Thor kept the giants at bay.

One of the funnier of these stories is the tale of Thrym. Thrym was a giant who desired to marry Freyja. To try to achieve this, he stole Thor's hammer and used it to blackmail the gods. Freyja, a strong-willed figure, still refused to marry Thrym, so Thor, desperate to regain his hammer, dressed up as Freyja and went off to Jotunheim with Loki

▶ *Thor fishing with the giant Hymir. This carving from a 10th-century stone cross at Gosforth in Cumbria, depicts the scene from the* Edda *where Thor fished for the World Serpent. Despite the pagan beliefs enshrined in these stories it was common for images from them to be depicted on Christian monuments and churches — either as part of encouraging pagans into the Christian fold gradually, or perhaps out of a belief that depicting pagan myths in a Christian surrounding emphasised the control of Christianity over paganism.*

disguised as his handmaiden. The dinner table exchange between Thrym and Loki is hilarious. Thor has distinctive fiery eyes, but Loki explains them as bloodshot, because Freyja has not slept! When Thor, typically, stuffs food into himself in a very unfeminine way, Loki explains that Freyja was so excited about marrying Thrym that she hadn't eaten in days. After this clever ruse is enacted, Thor regains his hammer and fights his way out.

▶ *Statuette of the god Frey from Rällinge, Sweden. Frey and Freyja are twin gods, male and female. Their father was the god Njord. The early Germans had a special earth deity called Nerthus. By the Viking Age, however, Nerthus had vanished and Njørd (who is either Nerthus transformed into a male, or a forgotten twin) and his twin children have taken on the fertility role. Adam of Bremen in the 11th century, described the statue of Frey at Uppsala as equipped with a huge penis — an object of worship and sacrifice before weddings.*

The Myth of
Thor and the World Serpent

One day Thor met the giant Hymir. Hymir did not recognise Thor as being one of the Æsir, though he was shocked when Thor managed to eat two whole oxen for dinner! When Hymir observed that if Thor continued eating at such a rate they would soon run out of food, Thor offered to take the giant fishing. Hymir was unimpressed by Thor's size and appearance and doubted he would make much of a fisherman — until Thor took the oars and, with his superhuman strength, drove the boat at terrifying speed into the domain of the World Serpent.

Thor was not afraid of the World Serpent. Disregarding Hymir's pleas, Thor baited his hook with the head of an ox and started fishing. The serpent of course took his bait, and Thor on this occasion got the upper hand on the serpent, for as it tried to spit out the head, the hook caught in the roof of the World Serpent's mouth. It pulled hard on the line and Thor's knuckles were grazed on the gunwale of the boat. This hurt Thor and made him angry. He exerted all his strength, until his feet went through the bottom of the boat and he was standing on the seabed! He pulled until the head of the World Serpent was level with his and the two were locked in each others' fearsome gaze. But Hymir was so terrified that he cut the line.

As the World Serpent fled, Thor threw his hammer after it — some say he struck off the World Serpent's head. But this can't be true, as the World Serpent must still be wrapped around the Earth.

☙ *Goddesses — Love and Loss* ❧

Whereas some of the myths are quite human in their drama and others quite possibly the result of contact with Christianity, many of the myths show their origins in fertility rituals and the basic needs of an agricultural life. Frey and Freya, the twin members of the Vanir who are the patrons of natural plenty and sexual fertility, and thus of love, were also very popular for folk worship.

Goddesses feature in individual myths where each one has lost her fertility symbol and great hardship results from this loss. Thus, Sif (the wife of Thor) has her golden hair cut off by Loki and is shamed until it is replaced by magic hair of real gold made by the dwarfs. Freya's necklace Brisingamen is stolen by Loki, and is later returned to her by Heimdall, who battles Loki in the shape of a seal to recover it. This is very like the stealing of Persephone by Hades in

▶ *This pendant depicts Freyja, twin sister to Frey. She is depicted inside her marvellous necklace, Brisingamen. This necklace, her prized possession, was made for her by the dwarfs — in return for sexual favours, it is hinted. The depiction of Freyja inside her necklace may be paralleled by medieval gargoyles who are almost surrounded by oversized vaginas. This emphasises the aggressive sexuality of Freyja, which was simultaneously a cause of humour and of insecurity to Viking men.*

▲ *A sacrifice to the earth goddess? This man was placed in a bog at Tollund in Denmark at least 2000 years ago. The acids in the bog have preserved him perfectly. The ancient Germans would sacrifice people to Nerthus by pinning them down into bogs. People who were sacrificed in this way were those convicted for what the puritanical Germanic society deemed "crimes of shame", notably adultery and homosexuality.*

Classical Greek mythology, which results in such grief for Persephone's mother Demeter, goddess of agriculture, that the earth freezes over and nothing will grow until they are reunited.

Nonetheless, the Viking religion was not a "fertility cult" — any more than modern Christianity is a religion of the Judean desert. By the Viking Age, the mixture of urban and rural life had evolved these gods and their myths to the point where their origins in fertility rituals had been mostly forgotten, though the sexual imagery of some of the iconography has a timeless fascination.

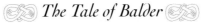

⊛ *The Tale of Balder* ⊛

The link between the gods and nature is also seen in the tale of Balder, which leads to the doom of the gods. Balder, Odin's son, has dreams of his death, which sends his mother Frigg travelling the world to exhort every living thing not to harm her son. So effective is her plea that the gods are able to play games in which they can throw anything at Balder without hurting him. That is until Loki fashions a dart of mistletoe, a plant so small that Frigg did not bother asking for its promise. Hod, Balder's brother, throws the dart and Balder is fatally wounded and dies.

In the poem *Baldrs Draumr* ("Balder's Dream") Odin seeks information from a seeress which might save Balder:

> *Hodur brings the famous branch,*
> *to become Balder's Bane,*
> *And suck the life from Odin's son.*

A common theme in European and Mediterranean mythology is the theme of a beautiful and beloved young male god who dies and is reborn. In Egyptian mythology there is Osiris, in Greek mythology there is the story of Adonis; and in the Middle Eastern traditions Baal, Tammuz and Attis all feature in various versions of this myth. The story of Balder, more than anything else, reveals the essential gloom

◀ *Thirteenth century carving from the stave church at Hylestad, Norway. In the story of Sigurd and the Volsungs, Regin and Sigurd roast the heart of the dragon Fafnir. Sigurd, on burning his finger and sucking it in pain, tastes the dragon's blood and gains knowledge of the speech of birds and animals.*

and fatalism of the Old Norse religious consciousness. For this god, who is so clearly a "dying and rising god", does not rise. In order to save Balder, Frigg has to get all creatures in the world to mourn for him. One person, an old giantess called Thokk, refuses. It is Loki in disguise, and by this single refusal he manages to destroy the possibility that the gods could save the world from the conflict and misery that is the human condition.

The Doom of the Gods

The doom of the gods follows the death of Balder. Loki joins his three monstrous children, Hel the hag of death, Fenris Wolf and the World Serpent (*Midgardsormr*). With a ship crewed by the dead, and a force of giants, they attack Asgard. Traditional enemies meet for their last contest: Thor fights the World Serpent, which he had once tried to fish up from the sea where it lay encircling the earth when he was fishing with the giant Hymir, and which he had once tried to drag from the sea while he was at the house of the giant Utgard-Loki. They destroy each

▶ *Odin fighting Fenris Wolf at Ragnarók — from a 9th-century cross slab at Kirk Andreas, Isle of Man. The Manx slabs, predating our manuscript versions of the Edda stories by around three centuries, are important in showing that the Icelandic versions of the stories must be close to those told in the Viking Age. Odin is identified in iconography and in literature by having only one eye and being accompanied by his totemic bird, a raven.*

other, as do Odin and Fenris Wolf. The fire giant Surt kills Frey. The wolves which had chased the sun and moon, keeping them on their course, catch up and devour them — plunging the world into darkness. Surt spreads fire over the world and the flames devour everything. This cosmic drama is revealed to Odin in the poem called *Völuspá* ("The Sybil's Prophecy"):

> *Brothers will strike one another, and both shall fall.*
> *Sisters' sons will stain kinship*
> *Hard will be the earth with great whoredom.*
> *An axe age, a sword age; shields clashing.*
> *A wind age, a wolf age; until the world ends.*
> *No man shall spare another.*

▶ *Sigurd slays the dragon Fafnir, a 13th-century carving of a scene from the* Völusunga Saga, *from Hylestad, Norway. This is the same story as the German epic of the Nibelungs (where the hero is Sigfried). The brothers Fafnir and Regin fell out over shares of a hoard of gold which was paid as a compensation (weregild) for their brother. Fafnir turned into a dragon and took the gold, while Regin fostered a young man, Sigurd, who killed Fafnir by digging a pit in the path of Fafnir and attacking him from below.*

The Myth of Idunn and the Apples of Eternal Youth

Idunn, the Spring goddess, guarded a box of golden apples. No matter how many of the apples were taken by the gods to eat there was always the same number of apples in the box. These apples were given only to the gods and were the source of their eternal youthfulness. Others, such as the giants, wanted to eat the apples too, but only Idunn could dispense them.

One day Odin, Loki and Hœnir were travelling over the mountains and plains. They killed an ox and tried to cook it, baking it in the embers of a fire. Each time they kicked the embers away, they found the ox still raw. An eagle appeared in the tree above them. He said that if he could have his fill of the meat, the ox would cook.

This turned out to be a poor bargain. The eagle took both the thighs and the shoulders — the choicest parts of the beast. Loki was very angry and struck at the bird with a branch which stuck in the eagle's body. This had the desired effect of making the eagle drop its share of the meat, but Loki's hands were bound to the branch and he was dragged off across the rough ground, until he was bruised and cut beyond endurance.

The eagle — actually the giant Thjazi in disguise — offered Loki a bargain: if Loki would promise to lead Idunn into a trap, he could go free. Loki, never the most reliable of the Æsir, agreed to this betrayal of the Spring goddess.

He went to Idunn and told her that he had found a wood where apples grew which seemed to be like hers. Idunn, curious, went with him. The moment they were outside Asgard, however, the eagle Thjazi swooped down, grabbed Idunn and carried her off to his hall. But he didn't get what he really wanted, because she refused to give him the apples of eternal youth.

Meanwhile the gods began to notice that things weren't quite right: they were starting to grow grey-haired and were getting a bit vague. They had a conference, and after a confused debate (they were now old and befuddled), they noticed that Loki wasn't there — moreover, the last time he'd been seen, he had been walking across the bridge out of Asgard with Idunn!

The gods quickly found Loki and, making dire threats, ordered him to get Idunn back. Loki used Freyja's magic cloak of feathers to transform himself into a bird and flew to Thjazi's hall. Here he found Idunn all alone. To carry her, he turned her into a nut and flew back to Asgard with the nut grasped in his talons.

Thjazi soon returned. Taking his eagle form again he gave chase — but Loki reached Asgard just ahead of him. The Æsir, seeing Thjazi chasing Loki, built a huge fire from wood-shavings under the rampart of Asgard. Thjazi flew into it and collapsed to the ground, his wings singed. There, the Æsir killed him.

Skadi, Thjazi's daughter, came to Asgard demanding revenge. As a wergild (blood payment) she was offered the choice of one of the Æsir as a husband. Her choice would have to be made, however, on seeing only their feet. Skadi wanted to marry Balder, who was the most beautiful, so she chose the most beautiful feet — to her horror, she found that they were Njord's.

The gods feasted on Idunn's apples and all was well again.

The Myth of
Thor and Utgard-Loki

On one occasion Thor and Loki went into Jotunheim. It was very cold and bleak and they couldn't find anywhere to sleep. Then they found an empty hall. The earth started shaking, so they retreated into a back room where they could sleep in peace.

Next day, they were disturbed to discover that they had gone to sleep inside the glove of a giant, which he had dropped in the dark. The back room they had slept in was the thumb and the thunder which had kept them awake was his snoring! The giant seemed amiable, however, and offered to show them the way and even to share his provisions with them. This seemed a good idea to Thor and Loki — that is, until they found that the giant's idea of "sharing" was to put their provisions into his own food bag. The giant offered the food bag to Thor but, try as he might, Thor could not open it.

That night the giant's snoring was unendurable. Thor tried hitting the giant with his hammer to stop the snoring, but the giant only thought a leaf had fallen on him. When Thor stabbed him in the skull, the giant complained only of bird droppings landing on his head! The situation became most frustrating.

Dazed with hunger and lack of sleep, the travellers reached Utgard. Here the giant lord, Utgard-Loki, made them welcome, though all the time making patronising comments about the puniness of the Æsir. This taunting was too much, after all that they had gone through, so Thor rashly accepted a challenge to outdo the giants in feats of strength and appetite.

Loki claimed to be able to eat more than anyone or anything. So he sat down at one end of a great trough of food with Utgard-Loki's champion at the other. Before he got halfway up the trough, however, the champion had eaten the rest of the meat, the bones and the trough into the bargain!

Thor tried to drink Utgard-Loki's drinking horn dry, but though he drank mead until his head reeled, it was still almost full when he finished.

When Utgad-Loki suggested Thor pick up the palace cat, the cat arched its back and resisted him, finally being forced to lift just one of its paws slightly off the ground. Then Thor suffered the final humiliation of being beaten in a fight by Utgard's old nanny, Elli!

Dazed, tired and humiliated, Thor stumbled to bed. Next day, he left Utgard, but once he was outside and unable to enter again, Utgard-Loki admitted that things were not as they had seemed, that the contest had been "fixed".

Utgard-Loki admitted he had been frightened by Thor's strength and had used spells to deceive him into believing the giants more powerful than they really were. The champion whom Loki had tried to out-eat was not a person, but Fire itself, and fire eats everything. The cat he had tried to lift was the World-Serpent, whose body is wrapped around the earth — as well try to lift the earth itself! The horn Thor had tried to drink dry was connected to the Ocean — and it had to be said that the sea-level had noticeably dropped. Finally, Elli, the old woman, was in fact Old Age itself. And old age is irresistible. As for the giant who had led them to Utgard — he had placed a mountain between Thor and himself while asleep. Even Thor's hammer could do little but shake a mountain, though two square valleys in the hills nearby showed the marks of Thor's hammer!

Life in a Viking Town

No event has done more to transform the image of the Vikings than the excavations which took place in the town of York between the years 1976 and 1981. The site excavated in the street known as Coppergate uncovered a street with houses, shops and wharves. This was the first time the British public was to see an image of Vikings who were not destroyers of everyday life, but who lived as an urban community. The Viking town of *Jorvík* came to symbolise a new image of the Vikings, not as marauders, but as hardworking immigrants, running retail outlets and workshops.

The Vikings in York

Prior to the Viking era, York was a town of the Romans, and then a town of the Anglo-Saxons. It came under the control of the Vikings when Ivar the Boneless (so named on account of his being double-jointed) invaded on the 1st of November 866. An Old Norse saga says, perhaps a little fancifully, that Ivar was avenging the death of his father, Ragnar Lodbrok ("Ragnar of the shaggy trousers"), who had been killed by being cast into a snake-pit by King Ælla of Northumbria. Ivar went on to attack Dublin, but his brother Halfdan settled down to rule York. York was to remain a Viking settlement.

The Coppergate site tells us nothing of these events, however, as the earliest settlement in the Coppergate area of town seems to have been no earlier than the 950s. The remains from Coppergate reflect a slice of life in the town nearly a century after the time of Ivar. This doesn't make it any less a Viking town, as Norse immigration and settlement to Yorkshire had been extensive over this period.

▲ *Death in a snake pit. This carving from the 13th-century stave church at Hylestad in Norway, depicts the death of the mythical hero Gunnar in a snake pit. The Viking hero, Ragnar, is said to have died a similar death at the hands of the Anglo-Saxon king of York, which lead to his sons' resolution to conquer York and avenge his death.*

⊛ Evidence in Place Names ⊛

Where the Vikings settled, the actual number of settlers could vary greatly. We can see this in place names. In the French duchy of Normandy, for example, places of Norse origin will have names like Torville ("Thor's farm"), Grimeville ("Grim's farm") and Hacqueville ("Hakon's farm"). While the names of the owners of the farms must have been Old Norse, the actual language they farmed in is French since -*ville* is French for "farm". By contrast, the names "Thorsby", "Grimsby" and "Hakonby" in Yorkshire are Old Norse names:

the suffix "-by" is from Old Norse *bú* ("farm"). From this comparison we can see that the Vikings who settled in Yorkshire must have settled in sufficient numbers to maintain entire Norse-speaking communities, whereas in Normandy they did not.

A century later we may be sure that the Yorkshire Vikings were still speaking Old Norse. When the archeologists came to recreate Viking York in the Jorvík Centre, they simulated this Old Norse conversation by recording conversations between modern Icelanders, the language of whom is the closest modern language to Old Norse.

Importance of Archeology

Of course archeologists had come across Viking sites before the discovery of Jorvík, but rarely had these been explored systematically. Vikings were not regarded as generating the same interest as, say,

▼ *Combs, textiles and weaving weights from Coppergate. These objects are the common domestic objects found at Viking sites. Spinning and weaving might have been used to make goods for trade, but most weaving and spinning was probably done to provide clothes for individual households. The weights were used on a vertical loom to weigh down the warp threads.*

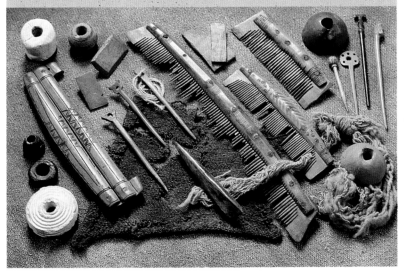

Romans. In 1970, the people of Dublin had to march in protest to prevent the Wood Quay Viking site from being destroyed before it had been fully explored.

To gain an understanding of the lifestyle and character of ancient peoples it is important that we conduct large, unhurried excavations. Through such excavations we can gain a complete picture of the site, rather than snippets of information such as had been gained from the "rescue" excavation of the cellars of two buildings in Pavement, around the corner from the Coppergate site.

Jorvík Viking Centre

The visitor to the site today sees the Jorvík Viking Centre, opened in 1984, which reconstructs a series of buildings in the settlement of the site. It is a long way from the dioramic display of the Jorvík Centre, however, to what the archeologists actually found.

Rubbish and Drains

What was found at Coppergate was basically a lot of rubbish, some drains and the remains of buildings. Viking sites have long been known to archeologists for the amount of rubbish upon them. This is not to say that Vikings were necessarily less clean than other peoples. Rather their economy worked in such a way that more waste was produced in one place and not carted away.

Coppergate was one such place, being a centre of what we today would call "value-added" activity. Raw materials would be brought to a site from elsewhere and then reworked into new objects, before being sold there or exported. The name "Coppergate" reflects the industrial character of the site. A name of Old Norse derivation, it has nothing to with copper or gates. It is the *gata* (road) of the "coopers" (barrel-makers). While this doesn't mean that every workshop in the street was a cooper's shop, certainly a lot of wood scraps and woodworkers' waste was found.

The Coppergate excavation gives a picture of life in one street of a tenth- and eleventh-century town.

▲ *Regin forges the sword of Sigurd's father. This scene, from the wooden panelling of an 11th-century church at Hylestad in Norway, depicts a scene from the mythology, but is also an industrial scene which would be typical of Viking Age York.*

The Buildings

It is worth considering what sort of picture confronts archeologists as they uncover such a site as Coppergate. What was found at Coppergate was a series of the bases ("footings") and floors of wooden buildings. When at different times the buildings were demolished or abandoned, the ground was levelled off to make foundations for new buildings.

At all times this site tends to be washed over by mud running down to the river nearby. As a result the bases of the walls and the floors, up to a foot above the ground, were usually simply buried and preserved by the time later buildings were erected. At times in the use of the site rubbish pits and drains were dug. These were naturally preserved because they were dug into the floors and the ground around and simply covered over by later building work. Things which were swept under the edges of the walls and trampled into the ground also survived.

What we are left with then is a good image of the spatial arrangement of Viking life, as well as the rubbish from manufacturing, eating and other daily activities. Indeed, lavatory pits were among the most interesting for what they could tell us about the diet and health of the Vikings.

Coppergate's finds are extremely well preserved. Because it is on a damp slope by the river, the site has a thick buildup of silt in every layer. On a dry site the buildup in each layer will be less and later occupation will mostly cut the previous layer when rebuilding is done. On a damp site, however, the stratigraphy may be several feet deep and less damage is done by later occupation. On a damp site, also, the water will exclude air from the soil and prevent organic materials, such as wood and cloth, from rotting. It is quite an experience to find a wooden post from 950 AD!

The earlier buildings on the site, which the archeologists came to last because they were deeper under the ground, were built from around 910 AD onwards. They were mostly of "wattle" construction: made by weaving thin branches to make a wall, with a thatched or turf roof. As all that is found of a house is the floors and the bases of the walls, there is a lot which can only be imagined.

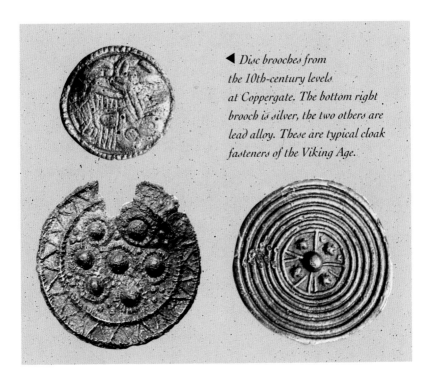

◀ *Disc brooches from the 10th-century levels at Coppergate. The bottom right brooch is silver, the two others are lead alloy. These are typical cloak fasteners of the Viking Age.*

Archeologists use a trowel to scrape off layers of built up dirt. In these layers quite delicate features are preserved. For example, we can tell how far the roofs extended beyond the tops of the walls because the water flowing off the roof scours a channel in the ground ("eavesdrip"). Doorways also tend to be worn down deeper than the surrounding floor surface. Archeologists use a surveyor's level to measure the relative height of the layers they remove and worn-down areas are easily identified by this process. In the middle of each house a hearth was preserved, surrounded by bricks and with a different clay and charcoal mix inside it.

There were two building phases represented at the Coppergate site. As the buildings on the site were owned by individual manufacturers, the replacement of the earlier buildings didn't happen all at once. By 1050, however, most of the wattle buildings were replaced by more solid timber structures.

◀ *A coin die, lead "trial" (practice) pieces and minted pennies from Coppergate. It was common in the Viking era for small centres to mint their own money. As most coins would be weighed it was often only a way of making precious metal into easily usable amounts, rather than official coinage.*

Evidence for Manufacturing

Among the many finds, the most valuable are those which testify to actual manufacturing activity. We have many finds of beads, combs, jewellery and coins from Viking sites. A site like Coppergate provides evidence for the making of these pieces. We have the actual stamps used to make coins, the pieces of antler used to make combs and some combs in various stages of the manufacturing process. We have the moulds used to make jewellery and the crucibles used to melt the metal.

There are a number of reasons why these finds are important. Many of these items are so valuable that they stay in circulation for generations. When we find the actual manufacturing evidence, however, we can date the event of the making of certain types of jewellery.

A Slice of Life in the Tenth Century

The Jorvík Centre recreates the life of the site by providing a number of characters with whom the visitor might identify. A jeweller sells his wares to a customer who is not in a hurry to buy. A young boy listens to sailors from a ship pulled up by the waterfront. Bones of dogs and cats were found in the Coppergate excavation so dogs and cats roam among the buildings. An unhappy looking man suffering in an outside latrine, screened-off by a wattle fence, humorously presents an important find from the site. A toilet seat was actually found in this lavatory pit.

Life at Coppergate must have been uncomfortable. Great efforts were made to drain the site and keep it dry, but it would have been an unpleasantly damp location. Skeletons from early medieval burials speak of the incidence of arthritis and rheumatism in this, as in most, eras. The damp conditions would also have encouraged respiratory infections. The buildings themselves were very close together, only around 1.2–1.8m (4–6 feet) apart, increasing the risk of fire and the spreading of germs. Around the houses, the dogs, cats and chickens fed off scraps and rubbish. This would also have encouraged rodents, though rats appear to have been less common in the Viking Age than they are today.

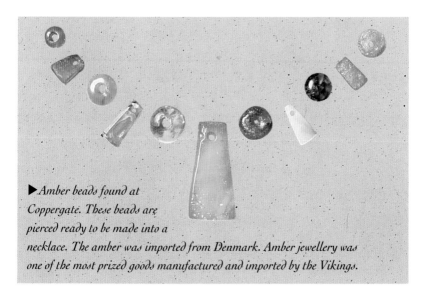

▶*Amber beads found at Coppergate. These beads are pierced ready to be made into a necklace. The amber was imported from Denmark. Amber jewellery was one of the most prized goods manufactured and imported by the Vikings.*

▼ *Weighing scales and weights from Coppergate. In the Viking Age it was difficult for the value of currency to be maintained at face value (i.e. what the coin itself was labelled). For international traffic in particular, currency was weighed and treated simply as precious metal. Scales were an everyday tool of the Viking trader.*

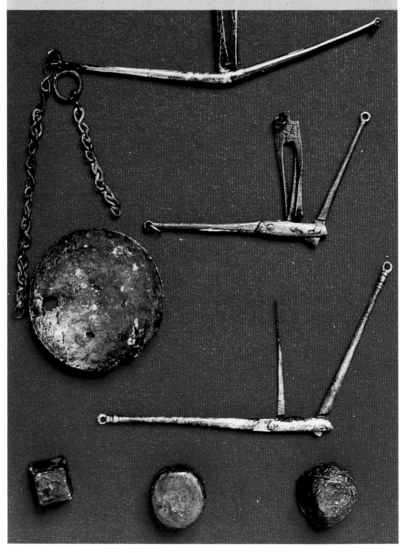

The dogs would have provided much of the background noise. If you visit remote villages in India or Nepal today, where there are no cars, the barking of dogs rises above most other sounds — especially at dusk. An Arab visitor to a similar Viking trading town at Hedeby in Demark, however, said that the singing of the occupants was even worse than the barking of dogs! This visitor, Ibn Al-Tartushi from Cordoba in Spain, painted a picture of urban life in 975 which may well have fitted Jorvík: traders locked in a commercial lifestyle, which was punctuated by occasional pagan festivals where animals were sacrificed, and revelry and singing relieved the drudgery of the daily grind. His was not a pretty picture and perhaps exaggerated. The occupants of Hedeby, according to Ibn Al-Tartushi, lived on the cheapest food available — fish — and drowned most of their children so as not to be overcrowded. We may suspect that Al-Tartushi was creating Gothic horrors to shock his urbane audience in Spain. Nonetheless, he probably captured the essence of this urban lifestyle, in which cheap living was a tactic to gain profits.

A Matter of Commerce

That these Vikings chose to live in such damp and unpleasant conditions reflects the needs of commerce. Coppergate, a manufacturing area, needed to be near the water so that goods could be brought straight in and out by ship. Any location further inland would be economically

▶ *Decorated bone strap end from 10th-century Coppergate. Strap ends were fastened to the end of belts to prevent fraying and to weigh them down. They were often highly ornamented in simple styles, such as this geometric interlace.*

uncompetitive. Real estate in such sites is at a premium, which explains the cramped quarters. At the site of Whithorn in Scotland, a Viking site was discovered in the dampest area of the site, by the side of the road leading up to a major saint's shrine. The Whithorn Vikings had clearly chosen to live in this terrible spot because of its proximity to the pilgrim traffic coming to the site, which they serviced with the medieval equivalent of souvenir booths and kiosks.

We don't know whether the dream of the Viking trader was to hoard up sufficient wealth and then move elsewhere — or whether there were Vikings who preferred a life of continuous enterprise.

▶ *Panpipes from 10th-century Coppergate. The only surviving pipes from the Viking Age, they were made by drilling a single block of wood. They can still be played today and produce the scale A, B, C sharp, D and E.*

▲ *Woodworker's tools from Coppergate dated back to the 10th century. Coppergate in the Middle Ages was the woodworker's street. This is a set of Viking Age woodworking tools from York and includes two chisels, a gouge and a shaping plane for shaping poles of wood, perhaps the masts of ships or house posts. Some of these tools are scarcely different from those used in woodworking today.*

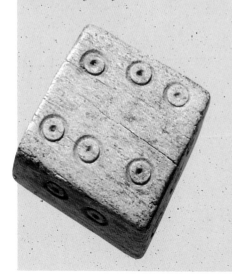

◀ *Bone die from Viking York. One assumes that gambling was a normal part of the Viking existence. Dice have been around since the early Middle Ages — this one was found in the excavations at Coppergate.*

"We are all Equals!"

When a Frankish king tried to negotiate with the famous Viking leader Rollo (*Göngu-Hrólf*), the Viking band shouted: "We are all equals!" But was this really true? In Viking society there were distinct social differences. Some people were certainly freer than others. The slaves, or thralls, were not the equals of those who went on Viking raids. And what of the women? Were they the equals of the men? Images of Viking gender relations often seem quite contradictory — a masculine life is idealised, yet women were not without power. Viking potentates in Russia were depicted with harems of slave girls, but the women of the Viking towns seem to have enjoyed a quite liberated status and were said to be able to divorce at will. Which is the real image?

◀ *Bronze statuette of the Buddha found at the Swedish trading site of Helgö. This statuette was made in northern India around the 2nd century AD, and was probably brought to Sweden in the 8th century. As it is not made of valuable metal, we can only imagine that it was brought to Helgö by someone who knew what it was. Perhaps a souvenir belonging to a Viking traveller?*

⚭ *The Ambition of Kings* ⚭

A lot becomes clearer when we realise that Viking society was not stagnant. Indeed, the Vikings entered history as a consequence of social and political change, in which new social ideas were coming into contact with the old, and Scandinavia was encountering an expanding European empire. The picture which we get of Viking society in the sagas is of a traditional belief in individual enterprise coming into contact, sometimes conflict, with the new ambition of kings who wished to set up powerful kingdoms.

▼ *Reconstruction of a Viking Age house at Hedeby, Denmark. Excavations of 9th- and 10th-century houses at Hedeby revealed dwellings of wattle and daub, and a variety of domestic artefacts.*

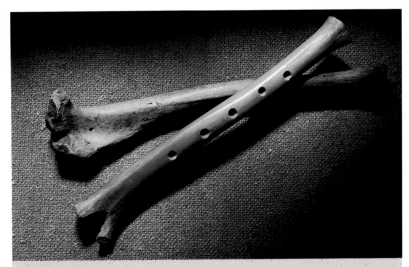

▲ *Viking Age recorder from Sigtúna, Sweden. This recorder was made by making holes in a hollow bone.*

The Frankish annals tell us that in the early 800s a king of Denmark, called Godred, fought to defend Denmark against incursions by the Emperor Charlemagne. It was Godred, or his immediate ancestors, who was responsible for the great linear earthwork known as the *Danevirke*, which cuts across the lower half of the Jutland peninsula. Godred took control of the major merchant town of Reric and, bringing the merchants under his protection, moved the occupants to his own enclosed town of Hedeby on the eastern end of the Danevirke. Back then, as now, "protection" was frequently a word for taking away the independence of merchants. We need not assume that the merchants necessarily wanted to be under Godred's control!

What did this sort of takeover offer the kings? Under the ancient tribal systems of Scandinavia, a king was not necessarily very wealthy or powerful. He had no absolute control over the finances of his kingdom. By taking over and levying taxes upon mercantile activity, he could gain a private income, pay his own soldiers and act independently of his chief warriors. The new, larger states which grew up in the ninth century and went on to become the modern Norway, Denmark and

▲ *Woman restraining a man — detail of a carving from a 9th-century wooden cart found at Oseberg, Norway. While we do not imagine that the strict moral code of medieval Scandinavia allowed much freedom for women, Icelandic sagas and Arab descriptions of the Rhos imply that women nonetheless exerted considerable social power.*

Sweden, did so under kings who rose to power close to major trading sites. In Norway, the new monarchy emerged in the Oslo district, with its major trading site at Kaupang. In Sweden, royal power centred on the Uppland area, near the trading sites at Helgö and Birka.

The changes which brought about the growth of towns were closely linked to the changing royal order. Those who lived in towns under the protection of the king could enjoy a sophisticated society with considerable personal liberty. At the same time, it was in the interests of the ambitious kings to restrict the liberty of the nobles who ruled the countryside, as this was a challenge to his power and a threat to his monopoly of trade.

It may be that town life was exempt from the more conservative aspects of society then as it is today. Special laws were enacted to preserve the freedom and safety of citizens. The *Bjarkeyjarréttr*, or "Law of Birka", was written to protect trade in the Swedish trading town of Birka. It set the king up as the protector of the rights of native-born and foreign inhabitants and visitors.

Personal Freedoms and Libertarian Values

And what personal freedoms did the inhabitants of the towns possess? Urban Vikings evinced a great deal of individuality. Al-Tartushi described how the inhabitants of Hedeby would use artificial makeup on the eyes, "so that their beauty never fades".

Like all people, the Vikings evinced a variety of sexual behaviour, depending on where they were and who they were living among. Ibn Fadlan, travelling along the Volga in 922, was disgusted by the sexual mores of nouveau-riche traders, who would have intercourse with slave girls in front of their friends. Such gross behaviour in frontier zones may contrast with the nature of the marriage power-relationship in an urban site, such as Al-Tartushi described in Hedeby, where a woman had the right to declare herself divorced from her husband.

Shoring Up the Social Order

The social system outlined in the text *Rígsthula* may represent a desire to shore up the traditional order of society in the face of rapid social changes brought on by large-scale trade, the rise of centralised government and accompanying growth of urban life.

In *Rígsthula*, the hero Rig visits the couple Ai ("great-grandfather") and Edda ("great-grandmother"). After Rig spends the night with them, Edda gives birth nine months later to Thrall ("slave"). Black-skinned, ugly and hump-backed, Thrall goes on to father the slaves.

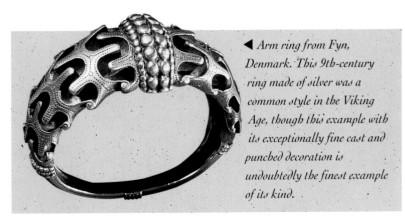

◀ *Arm ring from Fyn, Denmark. This 9th-century ring made of silver was a common style in the Viking Age, though this example with its exceptionally fine cast and punched decoration is undoubtedly the finest example of its kind.*

Rig then stays with Afi ("grandfather") and Amma ("grandmother"). After nine months, Karl ("peasant") is born. He goes on to father the freemen. Finally, Rig stays with Fathir ("father") and Mothir ("mother"), who gives birth to a fair-haired, bright son Jarl ("earl"), who goes on to be a great warrior and father of warriors.

The message of this tale is that one's social class should be regarded more as a caste and that this is a social order which is preordained. People rarely write such myths of a contented society "knowing its place", unless the social order is already crumbling.

A Strict and Conservative Society

Traditional rural society was socially conservative. People seeking an explanation for the raids and violent actions of the Vikings have often wrongly laid the blame at the door of Scandinavian society, suggesting it was overcrowded and permissive. The Viking practice of polygamy is singled out as a cause for overpopulation, and the pillaging and sexual promiscuity of Vikings abroad is held to reflect a lack of morality in Scandinavian society. In fact the opposite is true.

▼ *Viking chessmen from Scotland. Owing obvious debt to Norwegian styles, these chess pieces, made from walrus ivory c. 1150, were discovered on the Hebridean island of Lewis.*

The sexual morality of the frontiers was not typical of life in Scandinavia. Germanic law was strict, especially on sexual morality. This probably had the effect of encouraging bad behaviour when abroad, precisely because it was not permitted at home. Just as the behaviour of soldiers abroad today is often the opposite in moral terms to what is permitted at home. Most of the Vikings were young men, a subset of society who decided to fight abroad. They behaved in a way expected of some young men when abroad.

Men in Viking Society

Texts such as *Hávamál*, a series of sayings attributed to Odin, paint a rugged picture of manly activity in traditional Viking society. *Hávamál* exhorts the listener to "look behind doors for enemies", "carry weapons even in the field" and stresses that "fame never dies". But it is also hard advice, offered whimsically:

"No better burden can a man bear than wisdom,
... no worse than drink."

"One may know
but not another
what three know, the whole world knows."

"Give praise to the day only in the evening,
a wife when she is on her funeral pyre,
a sword, when it is tested,
a maiden, when she is bedded,
ice, when crossed,
ale, when it is drunk."

▲ *Hon Hoard, Norway. Dating from around 860 AD, was this a collection of hoarded wealth in the face of domineering kings?*

Fortunes to be Made

In the rough and tumble of this lifestyle there were definite fortunes to be made. Norway's economy was enriched by a trade which ran between the Arctic and the markets of Europe. Reindeer antler, walrus ivory, Arctic falcons and other arctic produce were collected by Norwegian hunters who travelled north in the summer and then sold their goods in Kaupang at the end of the season.

When King Alfred made an Old English translation of the writings of the Classical writer Orosius, he included an account of such a journey, which he took first-hand from a Viking named Ohthere (probably the Norse name Ottar) who visited Alfred in England.

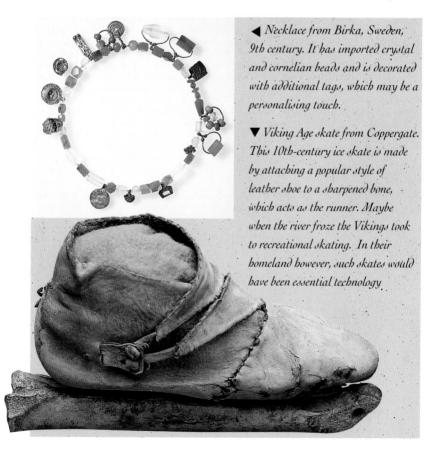

◄ *Necklace from Birka, Sweden, 9th century. It has imported crystal and cornelian beads and is decorated with additional tags, which may be a personalising touch.*

▼ *Viking Age skate from Coppergate. This 10th-century ice skate is made by attaching a popular style of leather shoe to a sharpened bone, which acts as the runner. Maybe when the river froze the Vikings took to recreational skating. In their homeland however, such skates would have been essential technology.*

Ohthere described a voyage to the lands of the Biarmas and Terfinns, where he hunted walruses and reindeer. This was probably the area around the White Sea. Ohthere emerges from his simple tale as a most enterprising figure, describing how goods might be taken from the high Arctic south to Kaupang — all with a minimum of fuss.

Trade Regulation

Freelance hunters and traders such as Ohthere were probably the sorts of people who held out against attempts to create a united Norway by the Vestfold kings of the Oslo district. The regulation and control of

▼ *Playing pieces from Baldursheimer, Iceland. These playing pieces, from a man's grave of the 10th century, consist of 24 plain pieces and the bearded king. A die was also found in the set. That a man was buried with such a gaming set implies that pastimes played a large role in the life of the average Viking.*

trade impacted heavily on the social organisation of Scandinavia. When trade was controlled by the king, those who traded outside royal licence could be attacked and their cargoes confiscated. Royal attacks on ships thus became "enforcement of the law". Private actions became "piracy".

The victims of this trade war were probably also the people who raided against the British, Irish and French between the 790s and the 880s. In this period, the sites along the western fjords of Norway show massive accumulation of hoarded silver and other precious metals. Were these reserves laid down to help ride out the economic oppression of the Vestfold kings?

A Conqueror for Love

The Norse writer Snorri Sturluson's massive history *Heimskringla* paints a romantic picture of the reason for Harald Finehair's desire to unite Norway under one rule. Harald is said to have fallen in love with a princess from neighbouring Hordaland, who was named Gyda. She would not be satisfied with marrying the ruler of a petty kingdom, so Harald vowed to win sufficient territory to impress her — and refused to cut his hair until he succeeded. Following his conquest of the Northern Isles of Scotland, to where many of his opponents had fled, he

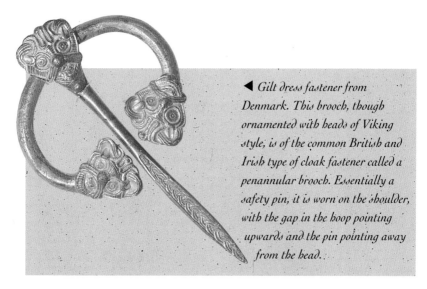

◀ *Gilt dress fastener from Denmark. This brooch, though ornamented with heads of Viking style, is of the common British and Irish type of cloak fastener called a penannular brooch. Essentially a safety pin, it is worn on the shoulder, with the gap in the hoop pointing upwards and the pin pointing away from the head.*

won Gyda's affection and had his locks trimmed by his follower Rognvald. He was named "Harald Finehair" thereafter — replacing his previous epithet, *Lúfa* ("mop-head").

Individual Enterprise

The Icelandic sagas depict Viking society as a dynamic one, one in which individual enterprise was central to status. Though the settlement of Iceland led to the foundation of a cohesive nation, this only occurred some 60 years after the first settlers set up isolated farms across the country.

▼ *Silver cup of Carolingian origin, from Hedeby, Denmark. The merchants' graves at Hedeby show that they were great collectors of foreign objects — perhaps as a conscious demonstration of their wide-ranging international contacts. There is evidence that the styles on objects of this type directly influenced Danish artists of the Viking Age.*

The early settlers were often rough characters. The story of Eirik the Red was probably quite typical. Eirik had been exiled from Norway on account of "some killings". This was a common scenario. Persistently violent or anti-social people were tried and exiled by the local assembly. The family of the murder victim might also receive a *wergild*: a payment to compensate for the loss of their family member. If this was not enough, a blood feud would eventuate — too much indulgence in this sort of revenge might also see people exiled. Exile was a severe punishment. A person in exile was a non-person. The thirteenth century Norwegian laws, in lamenting the rise of violence, made appeal to an earlier age in which the penalty for unlawful killing was forfeit of property and loss of all rights.

Iceland seems to have been too small for Eirik. In 982 he was exiled for three years for further "killings". Pioneers are probably frequently incorrigible characters of this sort. Rather than go to Europe for the term of his exile, Eirik was not afraid to spend three years setting up a farm in the great island to the west, which Eirik named "Greenland". According to the *Greenlanders' Saga* this "nice" name was a piece of sharp real estate practice aimed at attracting people to Greenland. Such is our modern view of real estate advertising, that most critics want to accept this story as accurate!

The Icelanders admired the individualistic nature of the founders of their colonies, as much as they admired cooperative activity and law and order. All of these elements were present from the beginning of the Viking Age. It was the conflict between these values that caused the Viking movement.

Runes

The Vikings were not a conventionally literate people. They did not leave us any lengthy written accounts of their exploits. Instead, the Vikings left behind them a series of brief, laconic statements carved onto standing stones, sticks, buildings and weapons, mostly written in an alphabet known as the "runic" alphabet. When not inscribed on formal monuments, runic inscriptions are also found as graffiti. The Vikings' desire to leave their individual mark in the places they visited is behaviour with which we can easily identify — or at least recognise as a timeless form of vandalism.

The Origins of the Futhark

Where did these Vikings learn to write? The runic alphabet is ultimately derived from Mediterranean alphabets, which some of the

▼ *Runes on a bone. Runes are commonly found on objects such as plaques, sticks and weapons — as well as standing stones and boulders. We don't know if the functions of runes varied according to context. Some scraps of bones seem to be for simply listing the alphabet, others may be "curses" or hidden messages.*

▶ *Runestone from Broby, Sweden, 11th century. This stone was "erected by Astrid" to commemorate Öysten, her husband, "who went to Jerusalem and died in Greekland". Presumably Öysten was on a pilgrimage to Jerusalem at the time.*

◀ *Found throughout the Viking world, runestones are perhaps the most striking of Viking Age remains to modern people. The commemoration of the dead by this use of literacy, in an otherwise illiterate society, demonstrates the need for immortality through fame which was so important to the Viking. This runestone is in Sweden.*

◀ *Runestone from Ed, Uppland, Sweden. Dating back to 11th century, this stone was "erected by Torsten, in memory of his father Sven and his brother Tore, who were in Greekland, and his mother Ingeltöre".*

▼ *Some runic inscriptions are long and very complex — as time went on they approached a fully literate form, with propagandistic messages and even poems recorded in runic script.*

early Germans learnt when they lived in southern Europe during the Roman period. The alphabet which we use, the Roman alphabet, is closely related to these early alphabets. This is why several letters in the runic alphabet are very like their equivalent letters in our alphabet, though usually written with straighter lines and fewer curves. The straight lines would have made the runes much easier to carve into stone, metal or wood — it is extremely difficult to chisel a curve.

Strictly speaking, it is wrong to call runes an "alphabet". We call our alphabet an "alphabet" after the fact that its first two letters are A and B — the Greek *Alpha* and *Beta*. In runic the first letters are in a different order. As the letters "f, u, t, h, a, r, k" begin the runic alphabet, the Vikings called it the *Futhark*. It was an "alphabet" in our sense of the word, however, and it is so similar to our alphabet that it is fairly easy to write English in runic letters.

The runes were therefore a matter of long tradition in Germanic society, as they gradually disseminated from their origins in the south to penetrate as far north as Scandinavia. The spread of runes did not cause a widespread use of writing as the Vikings regarded the spoken word as more effective than the written. Oral poetry was a highly

▶*Runestone from Gripsholm, Södermanland, 11th century. The runes in the body of this snake tell of how Tola put up the stone for his two sons "who died in Serkland" — a "southern" land —after "journeying east in search of far-away gold". Yngvar's ill-fated expedition is commemorated on a scattered group of around thirty stones in Sweden's Uppland region.*

developed art and Skaldic poems, rich in metaphor and complex imagery, were remembered generations after they were composed. One runestone, from Östgoterland, records a Skaldic poem, but this is rare. As for the power of speech: a rich and colourful insult was often the challenge to a fight, with insults seen as a way to deeply hurt a man.

There is much we simply do not know about the purpose of runes. It is almost certain that runes were only used for specific, limited functions, and not all Vikings used them. Sweden has many more runes than any other Viking region. There are none from Iceland and Greenland in the Viking era, despite Iceland's later reputation for literacy. Ireland has few runestones, but the neighbouring Isle of Man has 30, a proportionately large number. We can only assume that runes fluctuated in popularity, or perhaps "rune-masters" were not common to every country.

Runes — a Source of Magic?

How much runes were regarded as mysterious or magical has been the subject of controversy. Most of the surviving inscriptions are fairly mundane in character, commemorating individuals or events. In *Völuspá*, however, we are told that Odin sacrificed himself to gain wisdom which came to him in the form

▶ *Runestone from Maughold, Isle of Man. The Isle of Man has a set of runestones mostly associated with one sculptor of the 10th century — whose name is recorded in runes as GAUT. It seems that the erection of a large number of stones over a short period was the normal pattern — rather than it being consistent over a long period.*

of magic runes. Many of the commemorative inscriptions, likewise, come from locations which could be suggestive of ceremonial sites.

Many inscriptions from the island of Gotland, in the Baltic, commemorate Viking travellers. Why are they set up there? The pilot book of the Byzantine emperor Constantine Porphyrogenitus described Viking travellers who, having negotiated the dangerous rapids, made sacrifices on an island near the mouth of the Dnieper. Were stops on islands particularly a time to commemorate lost travellers? Was writing the name in runes especially significant in perpetuating the memory of the lost traveller? And why write the name down at all?

One thing to remember is that this was the only form of writing that the Vikings possessed and it was only sparsely used. It wasn't really a "code", as most people in Viking society couldn't read at all. Doubtless runes were seen as magical in some way, though the use of Christian formulas in some inscriptions make it unlikely that any mystical role they were seen to have was especially pagan in character.

When writing is used in a society which normally does not write it is viewed as powerful and arcane. The writing of a person's name in runes may well have been seen as enshrining some property of the person. Putting the name on a standing stone may have cemented a part of that person into a world which missed their presence. This is not especially magical, however, or at least it is a magic which still is seen in some degree in our use of gravestones.

Leaving Their Mark

Runic inscriptions are found as far afield as Russia, northern Greenland, and Venice (where they are found on a statue formerly from Piraeus in Greece). Only a handful of inscriptions are more than a line or two long. The rarity of long inscriptions, along with some obvious inaccuracies, make the lengthy Kensington runestone from the American state of Minnesota a definite forgery — though the folk of Minnesota are undeterred and have named their football team after their supposed Viking pioneers! Such forgeries as the Kensington stone represent a desire to make certain the Viking "contribution" to the regions they visited. They more reflect our modern idea of "making a mark" than any historical reality.

The desire to leave a mark on somewhere far away is sometimes seen in runic graffiti. It is perhaps fortunate that the only word to have survived from an inscription in the Hagia Sophia church in Constantinople is the name [H]ALFTAN. We are therefore free to fill in the missing words as having been an old Norse equivalent of "...was here", if we care to do so.

▲ *"Halftan ...was here". On a balcony of the great Hagia Sophia church in Constantinople, a Viking has written his name, HALFTAN, and a now indechipherable accompanying message.*

Death and the Afterlife

The Viking attitudes to death and the possibility of an afterlife are very unclear to us, for all that death was a constant accompaniment to the lives of warriors and travellers in the Viking era. Much of our evidence, such as runestones, burials and weapons, is directly linked to either the commemoration or the causing of death. Yet basic questions remain unanswered. Viking warriors appeared fearless. Was this because of a strong faith in a life hereafter? And why were Viking burials so rich and spectacular? How do the expensive grave goods relate to the beliefs of the Vikings? Were they for a future life, or just an offering along with the dead?

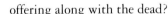

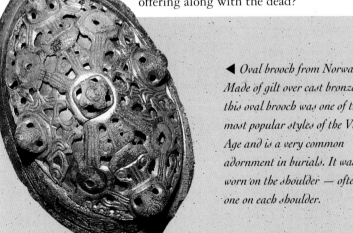

◄ *Oval brooch from Norway. Made of gilt over cast bronze, this oval brooch was one of the most popular styles of the Viking Age and is a very common adornment in burials. It was worn on the shoulder — often one on each shoulder.*

⊗⊃ *The Afterlife* ⊂⊗

Norse ideas of the afterlife are fairly limited. Warriors who died in battle were offered the prospect of life in Valhalla. When a warrior died in battle, he would be carried off by the Valkyries, beautiful women who rode across the sky above the battlefield. The warriors whom they selected were carried off to Valhalla, the hall of Odin.

In Valhalla they pursued what seems to have been the warrior's ideal of life. They ate vast amounts of meat from a boar which was slaughtered every day and was reborn for the next meal. They drank

▼ *This "Horn of Plenty", found in a Viking grave in Sweden, is a container for the most precious valuables of the buried man.*

mead which came endlessly from the udder of a goat. In between this orgiastic eating, they fought in the field outside, arising fresh the next day to start all over again. Not only did they wake free from wounds, but they never suffered a hangover, despite all the mead they consumed. Perhaps this was why this lifestyle seemed "heavenly"!

The Norse had another realm of the dead, Niflheim, the bottommost of the worlds of the Norse vision of creation. Niflheim was ruled over by the goddess of death, Hel (from which comes our English word for the biblical realm of Satan). Sometimes Niflheim is also called Hel. Though a dismal realm, Niflheim did not have the punitive character of the Christian Hell, and it is unclear what the life of its denizens really entailed.

According to *Hávamál* ("Sayings of the High One"), the greatest immortality of a person came through fame: "Cattle die, kinsmen die, but fame is everlasting". If fame was achieved in this world, perhaps Vikings were less concerned about the dull aspects of the afterlife.

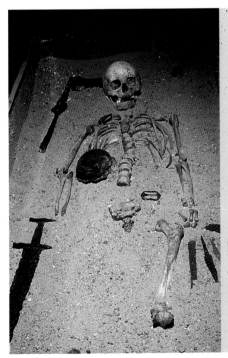

◀ *Furnished burial of a Viking warrior. This reconstruction of a 9th-century Norwegian burial contains (clockwise from left) a sword, shield boss, spear, axe belt buckle and arrow heads.*

Burial

The most spectacular Viking burials were usually ship burials. Ship burials could take a number of possible forms: sometimes the body was buried in an actual ship, sometimes it was cremated in a ship, or sometimes the burial was simply inside a set of stones laid out in the shape of a ship. The earliest ship burials found come from sites such as Vendel, Valsgärde and Uppsala in Sweden and date from the 7th and 8th centuries AD. This type of burial seems to have spread westward and southward into Norway and Denmark in the eighth century. One presumes that the spread of an aristocratic burial custom accompanies either the spread of people or of ideas. One possibility, hinted at in the sagas, is that a Swedish aristocracy took over some of the petty kingdoms in Norway and Denmark. In any event, the ship burial came to characterise royal burials throughout the Viking world.

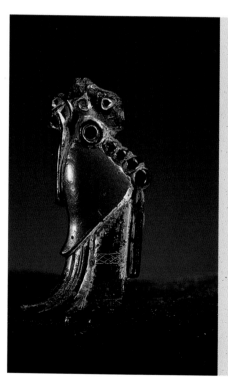

◀ *This 6th-century silver-gilt pendant from Sweden is thought to show a robed Valkyrie, as the necklace and bound-up hair are similar to depictions of Valkyries on the Gotland stones.*

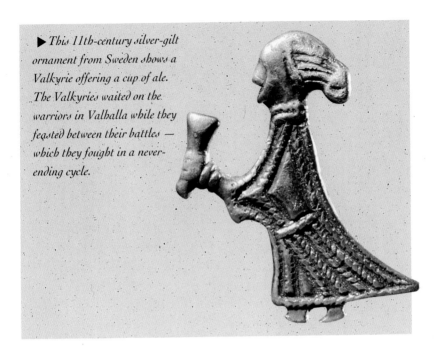

▶ *This 11th-century silver-gilt ornament from Sweden shows a Valkyrie offering a cup of ale. The Valkyries waited on the warriors in Valhalla while they feasted between their battles — which they fought in a never-ending cycle.*

An Arab traveller, Ibn Fadlan, witnessed such a burial on the Volga in 922 AD. He woke one morning to find the ship of the local lord drawn onto the shore. The body of the lord was placed in a tent on board and then the ship filled with many offerings: weapons, fruits, fragrant plants, bread, meat and onions, which they placed before him. A dog, two horses and two cows were cut to pieces and put in the ship. A female slave volunteered to have sexual intercourse with each of the lord's chief warriors. She then went on board the ship to be ritually strangled and stabbed by an old woman known as the "Angel of Death" with the assistance of the men who had slept with her. Then all the people came with flaming sticks and set the entire ship on fire. The story ends with a moral, typical of Arabic literature, that the Vikings value their lords so much that they speed their path to heaven, rather than let them rot in the ground. Viking burials varied so greatly, however, that we need not take this comment as being of any general significance.

Viking nobles often seem to have been accompanied to the grave by servants or spouses. When Balder is cremated in Skidbladnir, the magic ship belonging to Frey, his wife Nanna dies of grief and is also put onto the burning ship, then it is pushed out to sea.

In the burial at Oseberg, in the Vestfold cemeteries near Oslo, an ornately carved Viking longship actually contained two female bodies, one of a relatively young woman and one of a very old woman. This magnificent burial is perhaps the finest of all Viking burials. Dating from the mid ninth century, it is probably the burial of one of Harald Finehair's immediate relatives. Tradition would have it that it is Queen

▼ *Ship-shaped grave in Balladoole, Isle of Man. Ship burials might be interments, cremations on land, cremations on water — and sometimes, such as in this case, ship burials under stones in the shape of a ship.*

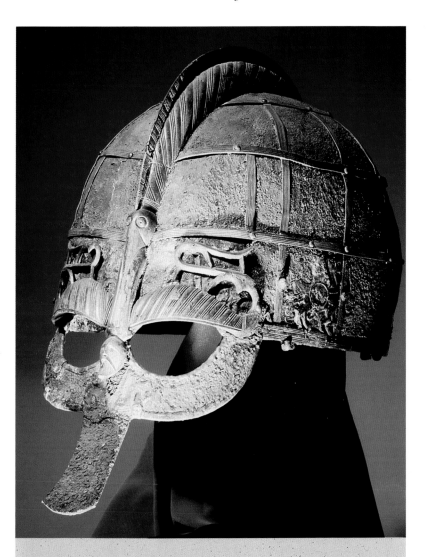

▲ *Warrior's helmet from Vendel, Sweden. The Uppland site of Vendel has given its name to the Iron Age culture which was predominant in Scandinavia, prior to the Viking Age. The Vendel style helmet has distinctive eye ridges and nose-piece.*

Åsa, Harald's grandmother. Since we don't know at what age Asa died, however, even if we were to assume that this really is the burial of Asa (which does not seem an unreasonable assumption, considering that it is a female burial), we don't know whether a young Asa was accompanied by an old servant, or an old Asa by a young companion. The old woman, whoever she was, suffered badly from arthritic feet, which were encased in sheepskin-lined boots — similar to those worn by many people today in defiance of fashion.

Sacrifice

Besides the sacrifice of these, presumably willing, servants, human sacrifice also was carried out as a part of religious observance. Adam of Bremen, a Christian bishop in Germany, described the sacrifice which was conducted at nine year intervals at Uppsala in Sweden. This was the

◀ *This cluttered picture stone from Tjängvide, Gotland depicts a complex scene with Odin riding his eight-legged horse (Sleipnir), a Valkyrie beside him, and a ship sailing in the lower frame. It is presumed the scene is a tale of a battle — with Odin a symbol of fate (i.e. death), the Valkyrie moving among the dead and the ship carrying the dead warrior to the otherworld.*

most important pagan Scandinavian religious centre, and contained altars to Odin, Thor and Frey. Everyone from kings and commoners was required to send gifts to this sacrifice. They offered nine heads from every available kind of male beast, and hung the bodies in a sacred grove that adjoins the temple. Dogs, horses and men hung side by side. Adam also noted that many unpleasant songs were chanted, so awful, he said, they don't bear repetition.

Icelandic sources provide us with savage images of Viking executions. One story has a Viking warrior executing a force on one side of the Seine, for the benefit of the other half of the same army, on the other bank. The image of "blood-eagling", where a body is split and its chest pulled inside-out, is a gruesome one, though how much this reflects real images of Viking raiding, rather than the Gothic horrors of Icelandic writers, may be questionable.

◀ *Wooden figurine of a bound man from Jelling, Denmark. Ritual binding of human sacrifices was a common theme in Germanic religion from the prehistory through to the Middle Ages — seen in the death of Tollund Man, Odin's self-sacrifice, and the ritual binding of the slave in Ibn Fadlan's account of the Viking funeral on the Volga.*

Viking Art

Dynamic societies produce dynamic art. In Viking Age
Scandinavia a combination of political change and increased
wealth led to a flowering of new styles in the 8th century.
These new styles, ornate, abstract and colourful, were carried abroad by
Scandinavian emigrants, where they encountered remarkable decorative
traditions in the Russian East and in the Celtic West. The result was a
multi-cultural artistic complex, which spread across the northern world
with Viking settlement and trade.

◀ *This harness bow, of gilt bronze
from Søllested, Denmark, is
ornamented with animals and was
probably for use in drawing a
ceremonial wagon. It is one of the
finest examples of Jelling Style art.*

Old and New — Dynamic of the Viking Age

Viking Age art in Scandinavia owed much to the common heritage of the Germanic peoples. A taste for colourful, abstracted images was enhanced by influences from the steppe peoples such as the Sarmatians and Scythians, from whom the Germanic peoples learned techniques of polychrome inlay, such as cloisonne, chip-carving and, above all, styles of abstraction of animal forms — what is termed zoomorphic ("animal like") ornament.

Such abstraction was not of the same character as the abstract art which has dominated the modern era. The latter is a reaction against formal, representational art and deliberately departs from tradition. Viking art was precisely the opposite. It was abstract art which built steadily and slowly on tradition. Newer styles had elements of the older styles incorporated in them. Such art was not meant to closely resemble nature, but was a matter of established convention, formal style and tradition.

▶ *Carved bedpost from the Oseberg ship burial — by the artist nicknamed the "Academian". With its conservative relief carving, this piece makes a dramatic contrast to the other bedpost from Oseberg (see page 26), which is in the dynamic new style of the Viking age.*

The burial at Oseberg, described in chapter 7, shows the strong link between artistic innovation and the social transformations which brought about the beginning of the Viking Age. The contrast between two of the bedsteads at Oseberg is especially dramatic. One post is only chip-carved. It is so traditional in style that the artist who executed it is nicknamed the "Academian". Another, however, is executed in a new, more vigorous style, with intertwined animals carved in relief, with studs embedded in the points of intersection.

Such a transformation of an old style into a new is undoubtedly representative of a new social and political order. For an artist to venture into new fields implies the existence of a confident new order, wealthy and with a desire to set a new image of change in society. The art of Oseberg is an incipient royal art of a new dynasty with big ideas. This "native" dynasty which represented itself as "uniting" Norway

▼ *The Oseberg Tapestry — a 9th-century textile which depicts a series of a wagons, thought to be funeral carts or perhaps the procession of the earth goddess.*

rather than conquering it, drew upon the old images and used them in a dramatic new form. The new style need not have been invented at the Norwegian court, but it is certain that it was accepted there as an image of change and a new ruling culture.

Fine artists such as the Academian worked closely under the patronage of the wealthy, most of whom lived around royal courts. It is really no different in our society, in which millionaires buy and collect the finest artworks.

Tools and Techniques

The technical innovation which characterises the Viking Age is also an essential element in this process. Just as in the case of the evolution of

▼ *Moulds and crucibles — tools of the Viking metalworker. The crucible is a pot of hard-fired clay in which the metal is melted. The moulds are also made of clay. These finds are particulary exciting for the archeologist because only the finding of such evidence can firmly date jewellery, which travelled far and was handed down over generations.*

ship technology, it is wrong to see this as the cause of change, though it is a part of the process. Advances in iron technology produced better tools, capable of finer carving. New techniques for smelting and casting not only produced finer weapons, but also finer jewellery and ornaments. Nonetheless, artistic innovation requires energy and ideas. All of these were present in ninth-century Norway.

Most surviving Viking art is applied art. A few textiles, probably wall hangings, survive from Oseberg. We suppose that some houses were decorated with murals and designs. While none of the latter survive, the ornate carvings on the type of medieval building known as a "stave church" (*stavkirk*) may provide some examples of a tradition of building decoration — especially as many of these depict scenes from pagan mythology, which presumably are based on older traditions.

Imagery and Symbolism

The meaning of much of the imagery of Viking art is now lost to us. Many symbols have religious myths behind them, which would have been known to the Viking viewer, just as the simple cross may evoke a knowledge of biblical stories in a viewer who is familiar with Christian tradition.

◀ *The trefoil brooch was the common cloak fastener of the Viking Age. This example from Ovre Eiker, Norway has beautiful filigree decoration.*

Most common in the Viking ornamental vocabulary is the serpent biting its own tale. Like the cross, this symbol is common to many cultures. The image of the serpent biting its own tail is a cyclical image: implying that all things really run in cycles and return to where they begin. This is also its broad meaning in Viking mythology, though specific stories expand this theme, where the world serpent was believed to encircle the Earth with its body. In one story, Thor went fishing with Utgard-Loki and caught the World Serpent. In one of the two endings to this story, Thor's fists were hit hard against the gunwale of the boat and he lost his temper and slew the World Serpent. As the recorder of this tale says, this cannot be true, as this means the world would have ended and we wouldn't be here!

Another potent religious image was Thor's hammer, which appears to have been a popular image for pendants. Some craftsmen in the Christian era seem to have had an each way bet on the market, producing combined moulds for making crosses and hammers. Scandinavian literature made much of the similarity between the hammer and the cross. The Danish historian Saxo Grammaticus recorded a story of a Christian man who needed

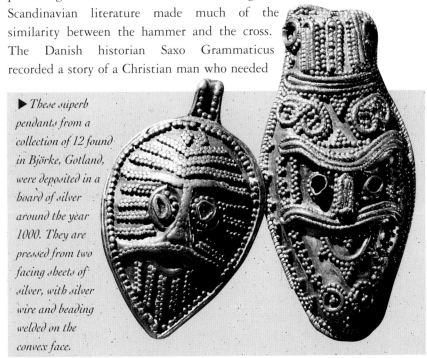

▶ *These superb pendants from a collection of 12 found in Björke, Gotland, were deposited in a hoard of silver around the year 1000. They are pressed from two facing sheets of silver, with silver wire and beading welded on the convex face.*

to attend a pagan feast. He did not want to reveal that he had become a Christian. When confronted with a plate of horse flesh, a sacred food for pagans forbidden to Christians, he made the sign of the cross over it to atone for having to eat it. When this aroused suspicion he explained it as the sign of Thor's hammer.

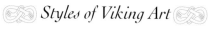

Styles of Viking Art

The Borre Style

Borre is one of the early grave sites of the Oslo–Vestfold kingdom. Characterised by its use of filigree (welded wire), gilt overlay and "chain motif" it was popular from around the mid ninth through to the early

▼ *Mårtens Brooch from Gotland. This gilt bronze drum brooch with panels of gold filigree is a superb example of the 10th-century Borre Style — one of the styles closely associated with the changes in culture brought about by the rise of the Vestfold kings of Norway — but also shows influence of the later Rigerike Style.*

eleventh century. It is found throughout the Viking world, including many examples from Russia and Poland, as well as in the ring chain borders of the exceptionally fine grave slabs carved by the artist "Gaut", in the Isle of Man.

Jelling Style

The Jelling Style is named after the royal burial site of King Harald Bluetooth, the first Christian king of Denmark. Evolving in the ninth century, it was especially popular in the tenth and was often used in combination with the Borre Style outside Scandinavia. The Jelling Style was characterised by distinctive interlocked beasts.

Mammen and Ringerike Styles

Closely related to the Jelling Style, the Mammen Style, also named after a Danish burial site, made more use of organic forms such as the tendrils which were also to be found in Celtic ornament. It also has larger and more naturalistic animal forms. This led quickly into the

◀ *Beaker from Jelling, Denmark. This chip carved silver cup, probably an altar vessel, reflects the Jelling Style of the 9th and 10th century.*

evolution of the Ringerike Style, which takes its name from a Norwegian grave field, and was characterised by longer, interlaced tendrils.

The Ringerike Style appeared around the beginning of the eleventh century. A carved slab from St Paul's Cathedral in London is of this style, and may relate to the period of Scandinavian rule in Britain by the Danish King Canute (*Knut*). Part of a Ringerike slab was also found at Coppergate.

Urnes

The Urnes Style is one of the finest and most evolved of the Viking Age styles. Rather than clustered tendrils, the curving lines of the Urnes interlace are more geometric, less organic, and of subtly varying width. The style is named after the panels from a Norwegian stavkirk.

◀ *The Lindholm Høje brooch — a fine example of the Urnes Style. It comes from a massive cemetery of stone ship-shaped burials in Denmark. it depicts an animal enmeshed with a snake.*

▶ *Urnes church — the Urnes Style takes its name from this beautifully carved panel from the 12th-century stave church at Urnes. One of the most naturalistic of Scandinavian styles, it is made of organic tendrils and serpent images.*

Art in Ireland and Britain

The Ringerike and Urnes Styles, with their use of interlaced tendrils, found an easy niche in insular (Irish and British) art. The twelfth-century Cross of Cong from Ireland shows a strong influence of the Urnes Style in the decorative panels on the arms of the cross. This is easily blended with the more conventional insular interlace on neighbouring panels. Scandinavian materials also had a strong impact on insular art, with amber from Denmark used extensively in the so-called "polychrome" phase of Irish art, in the ninth century.

Purpose

Use of these styles could be on objects as different in character as weapons, boxes, brooches, grave slabs, standing stones and wagons. The Oseberg ship had extensive carving on its prow, the Urnes Style is named after carvings on a church wall and the Ringerike Style is beautifully executed in a weather vane from Söderala in Sweden.

A frequent and invaluable archeological find is of "trial" pieces: carved pieces of bone on which patterns were tested and sketched before final execution on more precious substances. As much as in a modern art school, there were rules and conventions to Viking art — it is a great deal more than deft, freehand drawing.

The international character of these styles is striking and speaks of a common cultural basis to Scandinavian society. Regardless of the kingdom in which they emerged, innovations spread throughout the Viking world and were the common property of the Viking peoples. It many cases Viking art long outlived the pagan mythology which gave meaning to much of it and it is one of the lasting and timeless creations of the Viking era.

◄ *The Irish Cross of Cong, a cross-shaped relic box is a fine example of the blend of ethnic styles which characterised early Medieval Insular art. Dating from the 12th century, it has fine Urnes Style animals as well as Celtic and Saxon images.*

◄ *Trial piece from York depicting a pair of interlacing Jelling Style animals.*

Treasures of the East

I f the life of the arctic hunter was one way Vikings might make their fortunes, so too adventures in the East beckoned as a promising career move. The path eastward ultimately lead to the ancient city of Constantinople, now called Istanbul, but which the Vikings named *Miklagardr* ("great city"). The road to Miklagard lay across the Baltic Sea and down the Russian rivers to Viking towns at Novgorod, Smolensk, Kiev and numerous other trading settlements. This theatre of Viking activity has attracted less attention than the raids and settlements to the west, but it is equally significant. The Vikings in the East seem to have enjoyed the richest and most dramatic life of all Viking entrepreneurs.

The Rhos

The Viking expansion eastward into Russia, Poland and the Eastern Mediterranean began around the same time that the first Viking raids upon western Europe were taking place. The origins of this eastward push are less well documented than the raids upon western Europe, though archeological evidence indicates that raiding and settlement had begun at least as early as the beginning of the ninth century.

According to Russian sources, the Vikings first arrived in Russia when the Slavs "invited" them to settle in Russia in the 860s. A Viking named Rurik was said to have been the leader of the first group of Viking settlers. This story, in the Russian *Primary Chronicle*, does not, however, ring true. The chronicler Prudentius of Troyes reported that an embassy from Emperor Theophilius of Constantinople came to the

Carolingian emperor Louis the Pious at Ingelheim in 839. Included among their number were some people called *Rhos*. After questioning them, Louis found these Rhos to be "of the race of Swedes". As Louis' territories had been extensively damaged by Viking raiding, he was not too keen to welcome such emissaries, though he was obliged to offer them protection.

The Rhos (or *Rus*), were mostly Swedish Vikings. The above episode shows that they had began to settle in Russia as early as the 830s. The Rhos set up trade routes along the principal rivers lying between the Black Sea and the Baltic, especially the Dnieper, the Volga and the Vistula.

Traders, Not Governors

Though they founded and controlled trading towns such as Novgorod and Kiev, there is in fact little solid evidence to suggest that the Rhos either integrated closely with the local, mostly Slavic, population or exercised any national government, though they did control the major trade routes. The tenth-century Arab traveller Ibn Rustah described a very "wild west" image of society among the Rhos. He says that they owned no property, but dealt in sable, squirrel and other furs, and "carried their money in their belts".

The River Routes of the Rhos

One of the most remarkable documents to describe the life of the Rhos is an account of the sea routes in and around the Byzantine Empire, written in Greek by the tenth-century Emperor Constantine Porphyrogenitus. This book described the routes taken by the journeys of the Rhos to Constantinople from as far away as Novgorod and Smolensk.

The cataracts along the river Dnieper are described one by one. The Rhos waded their unloaded ships through the first, Essoupi; the second, Oulvorsi; the third, Gelandri; the fifth, Varouforos; the sixth, Leanti and the seventh rapid, Stroukoun. The fourth rapid, Aeifor, the largest, was impassable, and required a 9.6km (six mile) journey around by land, the traders dragging their ships overland, or carrying them on their shoulders.

▼ *The Pilsgärd Stone — this 9th-century runestone commemorates a Viking who "went far into Aifur". Aifur was the largest and most dangerous of the cataracts on the river Dneiper, in Russia. Stories of Vikings who died far away are common on runestones which shows how much the adventure abroad was central to Viking life.*

At least five of these cataract names are Old Norse in origin — and they are very dramatic names, too.

> Essoupi (ON: *supa*) "Sipping/Drinking"
> Oulvorsi (ON: *holmfors*): "Island-cataract"
> Gelandri (ON: *gællandi*): "Yelling"
> Aeifor (ON: *eiforr*): "Always-fierce"
> Leanti (ON: *leiandi*): "Seething".

Aeifor must have been notorious. A memorial stone at Pilsgärd, on the Baltic island or Gotland, commemorates the loss of a beloved brother with his companions. "They went far into Aifur". When they had negotiated these cataracts, the Rhos would stop to make sacrifices on an island (probably St Gregory's Island at Khortitsa) before proceeding to Constantinople.

▼ *These items are from a find at Staraya Ladoga. The bone artefacts and shoe in this picture illustrate the international urban culture and economy of the Vikings in the 10th and 11th centuries. These items could come from any Viking town in Scandinavia, Britain or Ireland in the same period.*

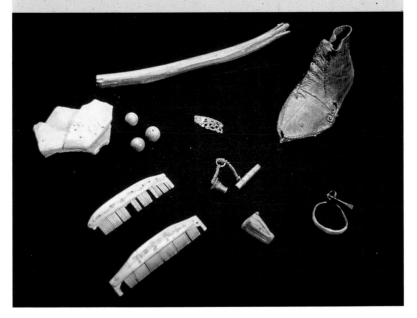

The image in this account, as in the Arab reports, is of a Viking population with continuing Scandinavian customs and language. This picture is less reflected in the archeological record, where distinctive Scandinavian finds are so far rarer than they are in the west, but there are possible explanations for this. Ibn Fadlan's account of the Viking ship-funeral is unmatched by any archeological finds, but we must recall that it was a cremation, not a burial. There is also the context of finds to be considered. Viking developments at Novgorod and Staraya Ladoga have been discovered in the process of Soviet urban redevelopment. The most distinctive Viking finds, however, have been found at sites such as Gnezdovo, where Viking burial mounds exist on

▼ *The Cammin Casket from Pomerania. This casket of elk ivory over wood is inscribed with complex animals and tendrils in the Mammen style. This photograph is of a replica — the original casket was destroyed in WWII.*

the opposite side of the river from the main town. Rare finds such as these seem to hint at a largely separate Viking population in the early period of settlement. It may be that the failure to discover obviously Scandinavian finds reflects accidents of archeology.

Viking Towns in Russia

A number of the settlements along the river routes have been excavated. The town of Novgorod has revealed an extensive sequence of Viking Age activity, with deep deposits in ground so damp that layer after layer of logs were laid down to make roads. This choice of a damp site is sufficient testimony to the desire to be by the water at all costs, as close as possible to the trading routes.

▼ *The Borucin Hoard from Poland is a 10th-century hoard of silver necklaces and beads from a variety of sources. The animal-headed chain is Scandinavian, some of the beads are Russian, others eastern in origin.*

▲ *Byzantine and Islamic coins found in Norway.*

The need to exert political control is another question. The role of the Vikings in the rise of a "Russian" state is controversial, though certainly "Russia" is a name derived from *Rhos*. The spread of Orthodox Christianity into Russia from Constantinople seems to have coincided with the setting up of some duchies in which rulers of Viking ethnic origin took control. The state of Kiev (modern Ukraine) is a case in point. What such states really owed to Scandinavian culture, however, apart from a trading economy, is debatable. The desire of the Slavic *Primary Chronicle* to set up the legendary Ruric as a figure who brought order to the chaotic Slavic tribes may owe more to later political mythology than any real Viking role in ninth-century politics. Much of the truth is obscured by nationalist and ideological toing and froing between Scandinavian and Soviet historians in 1950s and 1960s.

The Varangian Guard

The other dramatic role of the eastern route was to convey mercenaries from Scandinavia to serve in the private army of the Byzantine emperor.

The Byzantine emperor was a very different emperor to his north-western European counterpart. When the Roman Empire fell in the West, the eastern portion continued to be ruled from the imperial capital in Constantinople, until it ultimately fell to the Turks in the 1450s. Without the dependency of the western emperors upon the feudal bonds of obligation and support, the Byzantine emperors were aloof and independently wealthy, dazzling their visitors with their immense reserves of treasure and the pomp and ceremony of their court. The tenth-century emissary Luitiprand of Cremona witnessed the "pay days" where the emperor made vast payments to secure the loyalty of his generals.

In this climate of such wealth and few bonds of obligation — but a desperate need for absolute loyalty — the emperors recruited more or less private armies from populations outside their realms. The Varangian Guard of the emperor was of this type, being largely made up of northern Europeans: Saxons, Franks and, especially, Swedes and Norwegians.

❦ *A Famous Varangian* ❦

Snorri Sturluson, in the *Heimskringla*, describes how Harald Hardradi ("of the hard language"), travelled south to join the army of Empress Zoe the Great and Michael Catalactus. Serving in galleys in the Aegean, Harald's own men formed a separate company, ultimately becoming the core of the Varangian Guard in his era.

The Greek *Strategicon* of the 1070s records Harald's progress beginning with his arrival with 500 warriors and his promotion to the

▼ *Arabic coins from a 10th-century Swedish grave. These coins are an eloquent statement of the far-flung connections of Viking exchange.*

rank of *manglavites*, following the conquest of Sicily, and promotion to the rank of *spatharocandidates*, after a raid on Bulgaria. These ranks were levels of status among court officials. Circumstantial evidence indicates that the *spatharocandidates* was around the sixth rung of nobles (out of fourteen grades) and as high as any Varangian reached until that time.

Harald would initially have had to purchase his way into the army. Once in, however, the potential benefits would have been great. The Norman Crusader Bohemund of Taranto was offered a whole room full of treasure by the Byzantine emperor, to secure his loyalty. Though wages were high, bonuses were also often forthcoming. Snorri wrote that the amount of treasure Harald sent back to Norway was "so great that no-one in northern lands had seen the like in possession of one man".

Warriors and traders were not the only travellers to come from the east to Norway. Ari Thorgilsson records the visit of Orthodox Armenian (*Emskur*) bishops to Iceland, perhaps as a result of the links established by Harald.

"Savage and Irredeemably Pagan"

S tarting with conversion of Denmark in the mid ninth century, the conversion to Christianity of the Viking lands was a swift process. Even Iceland and Greenland, those most far-flung and independent of Viking nations, were converted by around 1000 AD. Why did the pagan Vikings convert to Christianity? The message of Viking religion, expressed in texts such as *Hávamál*, was hard, but practical. The morality of Viking religion was enshrined in tales of conflict between power groups who maintained a cosmic balance. The religion of the Vikings thus seemed to offer everything that a rural, warrior culture would have needed to justify its values and its behaviour. Christianity was a very different religion, with a different message.

◀ *Soapstone mould from Trendgaarden in Denmark. With recesses for casting both Christian crosses and a Thor's hammer, this mould demonstrates entrepreneurial acumen — as well as showing how a change of religion might initially mean little more than a change of symbols.*

⟨⟨⟨ *Persistent Missionaries* ⟩⟩⟩

The spread of Christianity began in the trading towns where, as we have seen, a more cosmopolitan culture had emerged than existed among rural Scandinavians. The missionary Anskar laboured in the towns of Hedeby and Birka in the 820s and '30s. He had some initial success, convincing the prefect of Birka to convert, and building two churches.

Anskar had come to Denmark under the patronage of King Harald Klak, who had been "immersed in a wave of holy baptism" at the court of Louis the Pious at Ingelheim in 826. Harald's profession of Christianity might have been as much a diplomatic as a spiritual move — as Louis the Pious was a powerful emperor whose

◄ *Bishop's crozier from Helgö, Sweden. This gilt head from a crozier or bishop's staff is of 8th-century date and was made in Ireland. It is unknown whether it was the staff of a missionary bishop, or was at Helgö simply as a result of looting.*

empire was expanding to the borders of Denmark. Anskar in subsequent years received mixed support from Harald, and his conversion certainly did not cause a broader shift in Danish belief.

This sort of attempt at converting individuals must nevertheless have laid a basis for the large scale conversion of Scandinavia which occurred in the tenth century. These earlier conversions at least made Christianity a recognised religion. The numbers converted were small, however, in national terms.

As in the case of the movement toward centralised kingship in the ninth century, we should view the Christianisation of the Viking world

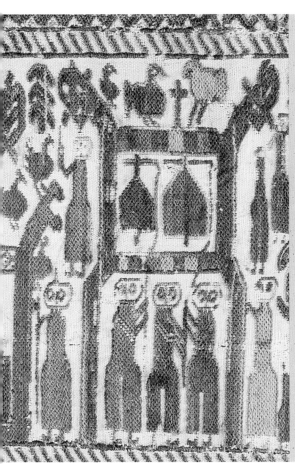

◄ *Twelfth-century tapestry from Skog church, Hålsingland, Sweden. It is thought to depict the struggle between paganism and Christianity. To the left the pagan gods approach; to the right Christians appear to be inside a stave church, where they ring bells to muster Christians or ward off evil spirits.*

as a penetration of mainstream European culture into Scandinavia. It was often an opportunistic event. A king might convert for diplomatic reasons. He might convert his nation both for its own protection and to create a rationale for asserting his own control.

An "Each-Way Bet"?

Harald Bluetooth, the king of Denmark around 960, seems to have had a healthy respect for the new religion. When building his royal chapel at Jelling, in Jutland, he located it between the two burial mounds of his pagan parents. Excavations have shown that he was unwilling to let

▼ *The Jelling stone is a magnificent stele from the royal burial site at Jelling in Denmark. The picture on the stone depicts Christ on the cross — but with a hint towards the image of Odin bound to Yggdrasil. The runes on the bottom read "and made the Danes Christian".*

his parents go without the possibly powerful benefits of the Christian afterlife. The two earlier burial mounds were opened and emptied of their occupants, and two burials discovered under the church floor in the 1970s are likely to represent the reinterment of Harald's parents in the new church. Thryi, Harald's mother, was a Christian herself but Gorm, his father, was not. This does not seem to have stopped Harald retrospectively accepting him into the Christian fold!

 Women Converts

Women, such as Thryi, are depicted as having been particularly influential in conversion and the promotion of Christianity — though sometimes we may suspect that this was simply a literary formula which contrasted the devotion of women to the unregenerate nature of men. In *Eirik the Red's Saga*, Eirik the Red's wife, Thjodhild, retired to a small chapel some distance from the house to practice her devotion, as her husband was not supportive of Christianity. The remains of a small building at the site of Eirik's farm at Brattahlid in Greenland, some distance from the ruins of what seems to be the farmhouse, have been taken as confirmation of this story. When the site was excavated in the 1960s, however, the remains of Eirik's farmhouse turned out to be right alongside the chapel. We now suspect the thirteenth-century saga writer of having seen the layout of the site as it appeared before excavation and writing the saga to fit what he saw as a strangely isolated chapel.

The role of women in conversion is undoubted as Scandinavian nobles frequently married women who came from outside the community. Such women might well be Christians. While conversion was largely a "national", mostly political matter the role that these women played in bringing in Christian belief on a personal level was crucial to laying the groundwork for national conversion. In the Icelandic *Landnámabók* ("book of the settlements") it is described how Aud the Deep-minded took possession of extensive lands between the Dogurdar and Skraumuhlaups Rivers and set up a Christian shrine at Kross Hills, which takes its name from the crosses erected there.

▼ *The remains of this church at Brattahlið, Greenland is near the site of Eirik the Red's farm. It is traditionally associated with Eirik's wife, who is supposed to have had to move to it to escape her irredeemably pagan husband — though it is actually of later date.*

The Conversion of Iceland

The entire population of Iceland was converted by a decision of the Althing in 1000 AD. The scene is described dramatically by Ari Thorgilsson in his *Libellus Islendorum*. A German priest, Thangbrand, came to Iceland at the instigation of King Olaf Tryggvason of Norway. Thangbrand converted several Icelanders, and caused to be killed some more who taunted him. Clearly those who conducted missions in the Viking world had a "frontier" mentality! Thangbrand returned to Norway, however, claiming limited success. King Olaf, taking a hard

▲ *Thirteenth-century stave church at Borgund, Norway. Stave churches are very early Christian churches, which are believed to be modelled in part on the pagan temples of the Scandinavians. They are often decorated with images derived from pagan mythology or symbolism.*

line, threatened death to any pagan Icelander who came to his territory. This, if nothing else, clearly was going to hamper commerce and some Icelanders became concerned. Gizurr the White, one of Thangbrand's converts, and Hjalti Skeggjarson, who was in exile for referring to the goddess Freyja as a "bitch", undertook to persuade Olaf that the conversion was possible.

Gizurr and Hjalti spoke at the Althing and called forward men from the two different religions; each side swore that they would not live under the law of the other. Then Thorgeir, the Law-speaker, sat under his cloak for a night and a day and, emerging, declared that to avoid conflict there must be one law and that would be Christian law.

◀ *Statue of St Olaf from Gotland, Norway. Olaf Haraldsson (St Olaf) was the most revered evangelist of Norway. He died in 1030.*

Christianity in Name Only?

There is no assurance that Christians such as Aud would have welcomed the national conversion of Iceland at the Althing. This conversion was not the practice of a peaceful, independent religion, such as Aud followed in isolation, but the transferring of political support for powerful pagan gods to a "more powerful" Christ. It was also a conversion made to stave off the threat of King Olaf's intervention. Such diplomatic moves may have had little to do with belief. The local chieftains (*godar*) took over the role of priests, the temples became churches and little can have changed for some time. Thorgeir pronounced that abandonment of unwanted children would continue to be permitted, the sacred pagan dish of horseflesh could still be eaten and that sacrifices to pagan gods in private could still occur.

Nonetheless, the number of Christians already in Iceland must have been considerable for this conversion to have occurred, otherwise the division at the Althing would have carried little weight. Likewise Hjalti's jibe at the goddess Freyja may have been a sign that the old gods were now little respected — though the image and deeds of Freyja might have been challenging to a man's sense of power at any time!

Harald Bluetooth's Christian State

Conversion for the Icelanders was a matter of ensuring peace. For monarchs such as Harald Bluetooth of Denmark, however, it is likely that it was taken as another of many opportunities to create a united kingdom and impose a strict control over the population. Excavations of the forts at Trellborg, Fyrkat, Aggersborg and Nonnebakken have identified these "Trelleborg Type" fortifications to be work of the reign of Harald Bluetooth. Tree-ring (dendrochronological) dates from Trelleborg are in the range 980-981 and show the construction of the rampart to have occurred in Harald's time.

The Trelleborg Type forts, though differing from each other in size, evince a striking uniformity of design, which speaks to us of a regimented military ethos and sense of imposed order — the sort of

▲ *Illuminated initial from the 14th-century Icelandic manuscript* Flateyjarbók. *This illumination depicts the death of St Olaf at the battle of Stikestad in 1030.*

geometric use of space found in very structured military systems such as the Roman. Was this a "unifying" military presence which accompanied conversion? Was Harald's evangelism simply an opportunistic move to conquer Denmark?

Olaf Tryggvason

Norway's evangelising monarch was also something of an opportunist. Olaf Tryggvason, like Harald Hardradi, had won a fortune in Russia and the Baltic, and in 991 made war on England. King Æthelred, who unlike Harald was not *hardradi* ("of hard words"), but *unrad* ("of no words" — that is, he had no idea of what to do). This is the origin of Æthelred's epithet: hence he was titled "the Unready" (*unrad*). Olaf defeated Æthelred's army at the Battle of Maldon, immortalised in a famous Old English poem of that name, and extorted thousands of pounds from the English.

In 994 he converted to Christianity with Æthelred as his sponsor. With the money and this new faith, both acquired from the English king, he set off to take over Norway by purchase and conversion. As we have seen in his dealings with the Icelanders, it was not a gentle message he gave out to the unregenerate or those who opposed his will.

Olaf drowned in 1001 in a naval conflict with Denmark, no doubt in part inspired by his taking over territory won for Denmark by Harald Bluetooth's evangelising of southern Norway. Olaf's later namesake, Olaf Haraldsson, known as "St Olaf", followed a similar career, being baptised in Normandy and then returning to take over Norway and complete its Christianisation. The conversion of the Vikings was as much a process of internationalisation and the resolution of international dynastic claims as a matter of religion.

Before Columbus —
Viking Explorers

A round 986 AD, Bjarni Herjolfsson, an Icelander, sailed to Norway to trade. On his return to Iceland he found that his father Herjolf had migrated to the new colony in Greenland. Herjolf was one of the first to follow Eirik the Red to the new colony. Bjarni decided to follow his father to Greenland, though it was late in the year with winter coming on. He had never been to Greenland before, but such was the self-confidence of the Viking mariner that Bjarni was not afraid to set out into the unknown.

The *Greenlanders' Saga* describes how, having collected descriptions and sailing directions, Bjarni would not be persuaded to wait until the following year. He said that it was his custom to enjoy his father's hospitality each winter and he wasn't going to depart from this custom.

The First European Landfall in America

While sailing westward, Bjarni was disoriented by fog and a storm and was blown off course to a land not known to him on the far side of the Atlantic. The country was "wooded and with low hills" and Bjarni noted that it didn't look anything like the descriptions of Greenland which he had been given. He concluded that he had been blown too far to the west and so he determined that he would sail northward and east.

Two days' sail to the north they put into land again, which was here covered by tall forests. Bjarni knew this wasn't Greenland either as he had been told that Greenland had large glaciers. Bjarni's men wanted to land, to gather firewood and water, but Bjarni said they had enough of

▼ *Greenland fjord, Gronnedal. It was in pockets of land deep in the fjords of Greenland's west coast that the Viking settlers were able to build farms and survive Greenland's harsh winter, while staying close to the lucrative hunting grounds to the north.*

both and he was unwilling to risk lives unnecessarily. Three days' further sailing before a southwest wind brought them to a high and mountainous land. This place did have glaciers, but seemed to be without any habitable parts. They followed the coastline around and found it was an island. This was probably Baffin Island, in the Northwest Passage between Greenland and Hudson Bay. The wind took them next to Greenland, where Bjarni settled with his father at Herjolfsness.

Though Bjarni was not especially interested in his discovery, the Greenland colonists were interested in these new lands. This is not

▲ *Doorway of Stöng farmhouse in Iceland. Vestibule doors such as this were a sophisticated solution to the problems of retaining heat in the house.*

surprising when we consider that America had resources such as tall trees which the Greenland colonists could not grow. Some of the younger men also thought Bjarni too timid in not going ashore. As if the fact that he had managed to bring his ship back from a totally unknown land, without loss of life, was not impressive enough!

Leif Eirikisson's Voyage

Leif Eiriksson, the son of Greenland's founder Eirik the Red, was one of those who felt Bjarni had been too timid. Around the year 1000, he retraced Bjarni's journey to his first landfall. Leif built some houses at a site, imaginatively named *Leifsbudir* ("Leif's houses"), which has never been precisely located.

The thirteenth-century *Greenlanders' Saga* tells that Leif named this land *Vínland* ("vine land"), because of wild grapes which were found by one of his men. This story was in existence at least as early as 1075 AD, when Adam of Bremen reported that self-sown grapes and grain grew on an island called Vinland. If the story of the grapes is true, Vinland must have been somewhere quite far south in the United States, as wild grapes do not grow north of Virginia. On the other hand, the influence of Irish legends, which we know the Vikings were acquainted with, may be at work here. In the Irish voyage legends, a paradise was located in the western Atlantic, which was surrounded by a mystical cloud. Both the grapes and the disorienting fog in the *Greenlanders' Saga* may reflect the influence of these stories.

The grapes continue to provoke controversy, but there can be no doubt that the core of Bjarni's story, especially the orientation of the landmasses and the directions sailed, indicates a pre-Columbian discovery of America. Once the principal sources on this discovery became widely known in western Europe in the 1700s, there has never been any serious doubt that Vinland was in Canada or the United States.

An Attempt at a Colony

Members of Leif's family later attempted a colony at Leifsbudir, both the *Greenlanders' Saga* and *Eirik the Red's Saga* depict it as short-lived. This colony was weakened by interpersonal feuding and encounters with hostile *Skrælings* (Native Americans). One child, who was named Snorri, was born there. The colony was abandoned after three winters.

Apart from the accounts of this brief period of colonisation, there are few further references to Vinland, despite the fact that the nearby Greenland colony was to survive another five centuries. It would be surprising, however, if there were not other voyages to Vinland in this time which have simply not been recorded. Icelandic writers were mostly interested in familial drama, such as that which unfolded in the colony attempted by Leif's family. One of the two sagas, *Eirik the Red's Saga*, was even written by Leif's descendants. The saga writers may not have seen much of literary interest in short expeditions to gather timber or other goods.

Myths About Viking Settlement

From our modern perspective, we are inclined to look at America as a more desirable place to live than Greenland. Neither this modern viewpoint, nor that of the saga writers, however, is likely to accurately reflect the interest held by the Greenland colonists in America.

The Greenland colony was a small colony with only some 3,000 inhabitants compared to around 100,000 in Iceland. It was not a miserable place by any means. The Greenlanders were more prosperous that their Icelandic neighbours. Like the northern inhabitants of Norway, such as the enterprising Viking hunter Ohthere, they enjoyed a comfortable life in a temperate location, with a few hardships, in return for the profits to be gained from hunting in the Arctic zone to the north. There were no Eskimos in Greenland when the Vikings arrived and they enjoyed a largely undisturbed existence. A colony in America would have been too far from these hunting grounds and the Skrælings were a further disincentive.

A Viking Settlement Site in Newfoundland

Unless archeologists stumble across the site of Leifsbudir, archeological finds which show a Norse presence in America are more likely to reflect intermittent exploitation of the resources of the American continent than any unrecorded long-term colony.

Between 1960 and 1968, and between 1973 and 1976, excavations at the site of L'Anse aux Meadows, on the northern tip of Newfoundland, brought to light the remains of some eight long houses and boatsheds of distinctly Norse type. For the discoverers, Helge and Anne Stine Ingstad, it was almost a fairy tale culmination to a search which had taken them over two decades and must have seemed like looking for a needle in a haystack.

This was neither the first, nor the last, site in North America to be claimed as representing a Norse settlement. Most sites of which this claim is made are usually mistaken identifications. Norse artefacts are found at many sites in Arctic Greenland and Canada, but in most cases it is clear that the sites are Eskimo settlement sites. The artefacts in question are pins, ornaments and trinkets which have been acquired from Greenland, either scavenged or exchanged from Norse sites, and carried by the Eskimos to North America. In this respect, a bronze ring-headed pin, a glass bead and a needle hone from L'Anse aux Meadows, the only distinctively European small finds, prove little by themselves, as the Eskimos carried Norse finds of this type from Greenland all over sub-Arctic America.

A forge for the working of bog iron, however, with lumps of iron slag, could scarcely have been carried to the site. Iron smelting was a practice entirely unknown to the indigenous cultures of the region. It is finds such as this which clinch the genuine presence of Norse occupants. The buildings at L'Anse aux Meadows are further proof. Eskimos of the Thule culture, which was contemporaneous with the Norse settlement period, built a type of rectangular, stone-walled windbreak, which have often been claimed as Norse rather than Eskimo buildings. The types of buildings built most commonly by Icelanders and Greenlanders during the tenth through fourteenth centuries, however, had turf walls, not stone, with a distinctive bowed alignment. This type of building, known as the "Thórsadalr Type" after a site in Iceland, is the type found at L'Anse aux Meadows and is quite different from Eskimo buildings.

The buildings are substantial, multi-roomed and thick-walled — we would describe them as substantial farmhouses if they were found in Iceland or Greenland. The principal activity attested at the site was the

▼ *This reconstruction of an Icelandic farmhouse at Thjórsadalur is an example of the type of house which was found in the Faeroes, Iceland, Greenland and at the Canadian site of L'Anse aux Meadows.*

repairing of boats, with wooden dowels and iron rivets making up a large part of the finds. The site at L'Anse aux Meadows shows most signs of being a short-term settlement, however, for boat repairs and resource gathering. It is in a prominent, defensive position and has barely a few months worth of occupation debris. Radiocarbon dates from the site would date it to around 1100 AD. It is nonetheless not impossible that this is the site of the colony described in the sagas, as radiocarbon dates can be unreliable. The substantial nature of the buildings and the short-term nature of their use would also fit the story of the colony which was intended to be long lasting, but which quickly failed.

L'Anse aux Meadows does not really fit the description in the sagas, however, and on the balance of probability it is more likely to be one of possibly many seasonal settlements from Greenland.

Short Term Visitors

The finds from L'Anse aux Meadows are few and there are not many distinctive small finds, such as jewellery. This is not surprising as this was a short-term settlement, seemingly without a burial ground. Strangely, while this site has convinced all archeologists, its impact on the general public has been limited. Amateur historians and archeologists continue to publicise much less convincing finds. Forged runestones have been found in various parts of North America, the most famous being from Kensington in Minnesota, mentioned in chapter 6.

Some of the interest in finds of this type reflects odd types of nationalism, for example a desire to prove that the Vikings settled in the USA rather than Canada. The effect is inevitably the opposite: it gives an aura of doubt to a subject about which there is no doubt whatsoever. Even without the L'Anse aux Meadows finds, no informed scholar over the last century has seriously doubted that the Vikings visited North America.

The Vikings in the Arctic, Greenland and America —a Long History

The discoveries of Bjarni and Leif are notable, besides their prefiguring of Columbus's more famous voyage, for their matter-of-fact character. To those of us raised on epic stories of the age of discovery, the voyages of explorers such as Bjarni and Ohthere seem astonishingly controlled and untroubled. Norse hunters made journeys far into the high Arctic. Finds from Ellesmere Island, to the northwest of Greenland, show their remarkable range.

Some rather bizarre attempts have been made to depict the Greenland colony as isolated, rugged and inbred. Nothing could be further from the truth. The Greenland colony was kept in regular contact with Norway throughout most of the later Middle Ages. Finds from the cemeteries at Gardar and Herjolfsness show that as late as the fourteenth century Greenlanders had contemporary clothing and a fully European way of life. The advanced technology and command of conditions that this shows is one of the most remarkable aspects of Viking civilisation.

Trial by Jury — What did the Vikings Contribute to History?

It may be fairly said that the Vikings have been judged harshly by history. Is this fair? Viking society placed great emphasis on natural justice and the right to trial by jury. Yet their status as "outsiders" in many of the societies in which they moved, meant that they themselves have not always been given a fair hearing in history. As few modern nations identify their nationhood with a Viking contribution, Vikings are frequently portrayed as an interlude in national history, which vanished with little trace.

The Vikings were a people, not a nation. "Vikings" is not a term for a race or a country. They were, strictly speaking, only a subset of the medieval Scandinavian peoples — the subset who chose to raid and migrate abroad. In the last few centuries there has been a tendency for history to undervalue the contribution which migrants and travelling people make to larger nations. The Vikings have been historically disempowered for not setting up kingdoms which "lasted" into the modern period, but it is worth questioning why we think this is so important. We no longer live in a world which celebrates imperial values. We live in an era in which enterprise, mobility and cultural plurality are defining values.

∽ *"Normans" and "Vikings"* ∽

Many nations don't remember the Vikings as anything but unwelcome invaders, even where, in some cases, their contribution is considerable. In English history, the Vikings are treated as a "foreign" element. Yet they are no more so than the Normans. In 1066, Harold Godwinson, the king of England, defeated the Norwegian king Harald Hardradi's invading force at Stamford Bridge, on the Humber. Shortly after, Harald himself was defeated by William the Conqueror at Hastings. *The Anglo-Saxon Chronicle* refers to Harald Hardradi's force as *Normenn* ("northmen") and William's army as *Frencyscan* ("Frenchmen"). Yet William's people were *Normans*, whose Viking ancestors had settled in France after 911 AD.

The written histories of the Normans show that, for all that they were French speakers, they retained full consciousness of their Viking origins. The eleventh-century Norman history by Dudo of St Quentin begins with the story of Hasteinn, a legendary Viking who set out to sack Rome. He landed on the Italian coast and captured a town, by a ruse of pretending to be dead and his men convincing the occupants

▶ *Face from a soapstone furnace stone — from the beach at Snapton, Denmark. This stone, probably lost from a trading ship, is of Norwegian origin and may be a depiction of Loki — the small mouth represents the episode in the* **Edda** *where Loki's mouth was sewn shut as a punishment.*

◀ *This unusual 10th-century pendant from Östgoterland, Sweden depicts a warrior's head wearing an early Scandinavian helmet. The man's head is surmounted by an eagle.*

that he should be carried into the town for burial. The story concludes with the irony that Hasteinn was too provincial a person to know Rome when he saw it. In fact he had sacked a small town called Luna!

This same "Trojan Horse" formula would crop up again and again in Norman histories. The Norman Crusader Bohemund would be described using the same ruse to conquer Antioch (with a dead chicken thrown in with him to provide a more authentic smell). We don't know if either the Hasteinn or the Bohemund story ever really occurred, but they form a conscious continuum with the Viking past of the Normans. Though they were now speaking French, the Normans espoused their Viking origins as a cultural identity, or at least as one part of their cultural identity. And they equated the "tricky" side of their character with their Viking past.

Norse Words in English

Many Scandinavian words survived the decline of the actual speaking of the languages. The northern English dialects contain many words of Norse origin. These local dialects are mostly no longer spoken, but they still flourished in the last century. Few of these words have passed into "standard" English, owing to the fact that the London dialect has come to dominate written English. Still, in standard English we do say "egg", from the Old Norse *egg*, instead of using a derivation of the Old English *ey*. Some Scottish speakers of English use the dialect word *ken* (from the Old Norse "to understand") in the context in which most of us would say "you know".

There are a great many place names which are of Norse origin, even where we have mostly long forgotten their meaning. There are only three "ridings" (from *thridjung*) in Yorkshire: North, East and West. Though we might expect a "south" riding, it is no surprise that there is not one, as *thridjung* means "a third" in Old Norse, so there can only be three "ridings". In the same way we might note that it is natural that some of the "gates" of York are nowhere near walls — because the word is from Old Norse *gata* ("road"), not English "gate".

Vikings and Modern Nationality

The political legacy of the Vikings has been negligible. The few nation states established by the Vikings fared poorly in terms of survival. The Mongol Khan's followers dined on wooden planks while the Duke of Kiev was crushed to death underneath and Russia passed into Mongol hands. The Viking kingdom of York was absorbed into Anglo-Saxon England. The Duchy of Normandy struggled with its origins as a Viking fiefdom subordinate to the King of France — Philip of France was still holding this claim over Richard the Lionheart during the Third Crusade. It was inevitable that the Norman dukes eventually identified fully with their English identity — in England they could be kings in their own right — and played down their weaker Norman status. The Norse colony in America was short-lived. The colony in

Greenland eventually disappeared in the 15th century. Never large-scale settlements, they existed for the benefit of a few hunters and traders. Colder temperatures at the end of the Middle Ages and changes to trading patterns saw their decline.

One or two states celebrate their Viking origins today. The Isle of Man, a sovereign state of Britain independent of the United Kingdom which surrounds it, is governed by a parliament, the Tynwald, which takes its identity from the legendary Viking assembly of the island's past. We should appreciate that this is as much a matter of choice as a matter of cultural singularity. The Isle of Man, like the neighbouring lands of Scotland, Ireland and Wales, is also a Celtic nation — the Manx language is a dialect of Gaelic. That the Manx have chosen to identify politically with their Norse rather than their Celtic identity is a particular choice, which bestows an individual character to their nationalism. The Viking past is set up as symbolic of freedom and individualism in a nation which is a haven of low taxation and a centre for amateur motor racing.

Iceland, too, celebrates its Viking past for its freedom and individualism. The literary evidence of Iceland's Viking origins was central to the revolution against Danish rule in the 1920s. One of the first steps of an independent Iceland was to return to the Old Norse formula of patronymic surnames. An Icelandic man or woman takes their father's name as a surname, with the suffix -*son* ("son of") or -*dottír* ("daughter of"). One of the first steps of the new government was also to demand the return of the Old Icelandic manuscripts from Copenhagen. The Althing (see Chapter 3) is still the national assembly.

Though the Vikings were those who travelled abroad, their contribution to the growth of nationality in Scandinavia should not be underrated. The royal dynasties which defined the nation states of Norway, Sweden and Denmark as they are today, rose to prominence under the conditions of the

◀ *This aggressive looking carving of a man's head is part of a wagon discovered in the 9th-century royal burial at Oseberg in Norway. It is the terminal of one of the arms of the cradle which supports the body of the wagon.*

Viking Age. The regulated trade of the Viking Age was an integral part of the rise of the overlordship of figures such as Harald Finehair and Godred. Icelandic writers, products of a Viking colony which espoused little love for the Norse crown, worked at the Norwegian court. Icelandic writers provided much of Norway's "national" literature. Relations between colonies and their homelands are often dynamic.

▶ *This 7th-century belt buckle is from Åker, Norway. A common Germanic type, this buckle is decorated with chip carving and inlaid garnets. It is an example of the Swedish-centred Vendal style of decoration, which was dominant prior to the Viking Age.*

▼ *Ninth-century carved wagon from the ship burial at Oseberg, Norway.*

The Vikings and Medieval Scandinavia

Those who had lived in the colonies or travelled abroad enjoyed special status in Scandinavia. In the fictional Icelandic story of Audun and the bear, one of the most charming of the short stories known as *thættir*, Audun, a smart-talking young man, takes a polar bear to Norway and Denmark, which impresses the kings. Snorri Sturluson, a genuine thirteenth century traveller, enjoyed patronage from the Norwegian king for his writing. The Norwegian traveller Harald Hardradi, returning to Scandinavia a wealthy man from long service in the Aegean, simply bought Norway! Both the smart words of the Icelanders and the gold of Miklagard were recognised as having outstanding value in Scandinavia.

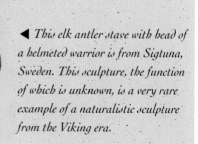

◀ *This elk antler stave with head of a helmeted warrior is from Sigtuna, Sweden. This sculpture, the function of which is unknown, is a very rare example of a naturalistic sculpture from the Viking era.*

⊗ *Our Judgement* ⊗

How then should we remember the Vikings? Their monuments are subtle, much of their image was violent and they are not easily defined by our standards of what is important and unimportant. Their mariners may be described as "intrepid", until we recall how unconcernedly they went about their work. We might call them a "proud" people, but "independent" is probably more the case. Romantics have seen in them images of socialism, totalitarianism, indomitable spirit and artfulness. The more one looks, however, the more they seem practical of spirit — which, insofar as practicality is often ruthless, can be both a positive and negative quality in our terms.

In *Hávamál*, we are told that fame was the most coveted form of immortality for a Viking. Did the Vikings, as a group, achieve fame? The Vikings were most of all a dramatic people. They appeared suddenly in European history, colonised localities both very central and very remote, transformed European economy and, following their decline as a distinct group, their Icelandic descendants reinvented their image with a unique literary art. They had matchless ships and weapons, a vibrant and dynamic art and a very self-conscious identity.

European culture is still finding the correct ways to acknowledge this unique people and their contribution to western civilisation. Our more inclusive age is an appropriate time to appreciate this legacy of Europe's most wide-ranging ancient culture.

Further Reading

K. Crossley-Holland (trans.), *The Norse Myths* (London, Deutsch, 1980).

R.W.V. Elliott, *Runes* (Manchester, Manchester University Press, 1959).

H. Ellis Davidson, *Gods and Myths of Northern Europe* (Harmondsworth, Penguin, 1964).

H. Ellis Davidson, *Pagan Scandinavia* (London, Thames and Hudson, 1967).

H. Ellis-Davidson, *The Viking Road to Byzantium* (London, Allen and Unwin, 1976).

A. Faulkes (trans.), Snorri Sturluson, *Edda* (Dent, 1987).

P. Foote and D. Wilson, *The Viking Achievement* (London, Sidgwick and Jackson, 1970).

P.V. Glob, *The Bog People* (trans. R. Bruce-Mitford, London, Faber and Faber, 1969).

E.V. Gordon, *An Introduction to Old Norse* (Oxford, Oxford University Press, 2nd editon A.R. Taylor, 1957).

J. Graham-Campbell and D. Kidd, *The Vikings* (London, British Museum Press, 1980).

J. Graham-Campbell, *The Viking World* (New York, Ticknor and Fields, 1980).

J. Graham-Campbell, *Viking Artefacts* (London, British Museum Press, 1980).

J. Graham-Campbell, *A Cultural Atlas of the Viking World* (New York, Facts on File, 1994).

J. Graham-Campbell and D. Kidd, *The Vikings* (British Museum Press, 1980).

R. Hall, *The Viking Dig* (York, York Archaeological Trust, 1982).

T. Heffernan, *Wood Quay* (Dublin, 1974).

G. Jones (trans.), *Eirik the Red and other Icelandic Sagas* (London and New York, Oxford University Press, 1961).

G. Jones, *A History of the Vikings* (Oxford and New York, Oxford University Press, 1968).

G. Jones, *The Norse Atlantic Saga* (Oxford and New York, Oxford University Press, 2nd Edition, 1986).

S. Laing (trans.), *Heimskringla—the Norse Kings Sagas by Snorre Sturluson* (London and Toronto, J.M. Dent Everyman Library, 1930).

M. Magnusson and H. Pálsson (trans.), *The Vinland Sagas—the Norse Discovery of America* (Penguin, Harmondsworth, 1965).

M. Magnusson, *Vikings!* (BBC, London, 1980).

M. Magnusson and W. Forman, *Hammer of the North* (Orbis, London, 1976).

M. Magnusson and H. Pálsson (trans.), *Laxdæla Saga* (Harmondsworth, Penguin, 1969).

G.J. Marcus, *The Conquest of the North Atlantic* (Boydell Press, Woodbridge, 1980).

R. Page, *Chronicles of the Vikings* (London, British Museum Press, 1995).

R. Page, *Runes* (London, British Museum Press, 1991).

H. Pálsson and P. Edwards (trans.), *Egils Saga* (Harmondsworth, Penguin, 1976

H. Pálsson and P. Edwards (trans.), *Eyrbyggja Saga* (Harmondsworth, Penguin, 1989).

P. Sawyer, *The Age of the Vikings* (2nd Edition, Edward Arnold, 1971).

P. Sawyer, *Kings and Vikings* (London and New York, Methuen, 1982).

G. Turville Petre, *The Origins of Icelandic Literature* (Oxford, 1953).

E. Wahlgren, *The Vikings and America* (London, Thames and Hudson, 1986).

D.M. Wilson (ed.), *The Northern World* (Thames and Hudson, 1980).

Picture Credits

Aalborg Historiske Museum
p. 104 (Jan Slot-Carlsen)

AKG photo
p. 11, p. 82, p. 122

Ancient Art and Architecture
p. 77, p. 80, p. 102, p. 139

Colleen Batey
p. 79

Bridgeman Art Library
page 16 - Trinity College,
Dublin/Bridgeman Art Library,
London
p. 28 - Musee de la Tapisserie,
Bayeux/Bridgeman Art Library,
London, with special
authorisation of the city of
Baueux, Giraudon/Bridgeman Art
Library
p. 20 - Musee de la Tapisserie,
Bayeux/Bridgeman Art Library,
London, with special
authorisation of the city of
Baueux

British Museum
p. 22

CM Dixon
Back cover, p. 76 - Dress fastener
from Denmark
p. 15, p. 19, p. 36, p. 46, p. 47,
p. 48, p. 57, p. 71, p. 81A, p.
81B, p. 84, p. 87, p. 89, p. 92,
p. 94, p. 96, p. 112, p. 116,

David Collison
p. 86, p. 111

e.t. archive
Cover background, p. 32 - Viking
picture stone from Lillbjors
Gotland, 8th century AD
p. 100

**Leslie Garland Picture
Library**
p. 13, p. 29

Simon Ian Hill
p. 68

**Historisk Museum,
Moesgard**
p. 67

**Icelandic Photo and Press
Service**
p. 131, p. 132, p. 136

National Museum of Copenhagen
p. 95

National Museum of Ireland
p. 106

Neil Price
p. 83

Andrej Ring
p. 113

Statens Historiska Museum
Front cover, p. 146 p. 74A

Ray Sutcliffe
p. 110

Universitetes Oldsaksamling
p. 73, p. 97, p. 98

Werner Forman Archive
Back cover, p. 42 - Statuette of Frey, god of fertility, Statens Historiska Museum, Stockholm
Back cover, p. 103 - Beaker, probably an altar chausible, National Museum, Copenhagen
Back cover, p. 145 - Brooch in the early Vendel style with cloisonne enamel work and precious stones, Universitetets Oldsaksamling, Oslo

p. 12 (WFA/National Museum, Copenhagen),
p. 21 (WFA/Maritime Museum, Bergen),
p. 23 (WFA/Statens Historiska Museum, Stockholm),
p. 25 (WFA/Maritime Museum, Bergen),
p. 26 (WFA/Viking Ship Museum, Bygdoy),
p. 27 (WFA/Viking Ship Museum, Bygdoy),
p. 30 (WFA/Viking Ship Museum, Bygdoy),
p. 35 (WFA/Stofnun Arna Magnussonar a Islandi, Iceland),
p. 40 (WFA/National Museum, Iceland), p. 41,
p. 44 (WFA/Statens Historiska, Museum, Stockholm),
p. 45 (WFA/Silkeborg Museum, Denmark),
p. 54 (WFA/Universitetets Oldsaksamling, Oslo),
p. 66 (WFA/Statens Historiska Museum, Stockholm),
p. 69 (WFA/Viking Ship Museum, Bygdoy),
p. 70 (WFA/National Museum, Copenhagen),
p. 75 (WFA/National Museum, Iceland),
p. 88 (WFA/Statens Historiska Museum, Stockholm),

Index

Acknowledgements

I would like to thank Peter Beatson for his work in the planning stages of this book, and Aedeen Cremin and Des O'Malley for recommending that I write it. Karen Jankulak and Kathy O'Halloran provided constant encouragement during the writing stages and Carole Cusack and Deirdre Wooding proofread several sections. I would also like to thank my colleagues in the Andfætlinga Samband at Sydney University for much inspiring discussion of Icelandic matters over many years. I would also like to express my particular thanks to Deborah Nixon for her vision and guidance behind this book. The Series Editor, Cynthia Blanche, and Project Co-ordinator, Jenny Coren, have provided helpful suggestions at every stage. All errors are my sole responsibility.

First published in the United States of America in 1998 by
RIZZOLI INTERNATIONAL PUBLICATIONS, INC.
300 Park Avenue South, New York, NY 10010

First published in Australia in 1997
by Lansdowne Publishing Pty Ltd
Sydney, Australia

ISBN 0-8478-2106-4
LC 97-76003

Map illustration on pages 8–9 by Dianne Bradley

Publisher: Deborah Nixon
Production Manager: Sally Stokes
Series Editor: Cynthia Blanche
Designer: Robyn Latimer
Project Co-ordinator: Jennifer Coren
Picture Researcher: Jane Lewis
Set in Garamond on QuarkXpress

Printed in Hong Kong by South China Printing Company